The Alchemy of Divorce

Embracing the Journey from
Heartbreak to Hope

Lana Foladare, M.A., C.P.C.C.

BALBOA.
PRESS

A DIVISION OF HAY HOUSE

Lana Foladare
lanafoladare@gmail.com
www.AscendantLiving.com

Balboa Press books may be ordered through booksellers or by contacting:
Balboa Press
A Division of Hay House
1663 Liberty Drive
Bloomington, IN 47403
www.balboapress.com
1-(877) 407-4847

Printed in the United States of America
Balboa Press rev. date: 8/25/2011

Note to Men

This is a chick book. Please don't be offended. If you are in touch with your feminine side, you'll most likely enjoy it and find humor too. If you're not in touch with your feminine side, give this to your sister or your cat, if she's female. I love you. The world needs you. You are valuable. And this is a chick book.

A book isn't written alone and I thank the following people for supporting me along the way. Thank you to the members of my divorce support group; you know who you are.

Thank you to my sweet, fierce writing group in Campbell, CA who provided me with unedited feedback. A special personal thanks to Laural Wauters, Pamelah Landers, Shazna Jai, Jill Mellick, Sharla Jacobs and Jesse Koren, Sarah Medlicott, Nina Price, Fani Nicheva and my fabulous community of coaches through Coaches Training Institute. Thank you Barbara Fagan of Source Point Training and the entire Seattle Leadership team.

I couldn't have done this without Andrea Glass, my editor who coached me and cajoled me to finish my manuscript.

Thank you to all those who have loved me on my journey. A huge thank you to my clients who so willingly shared of themselves with me. I also could not have finished my project without Pandora.com, Kings of Leon and Owl City. Thank you for saving me from myself.

And the biggest thanks of all to my daughter, for inspiring me to be the best me ever.

For all women who are learning to stand up for themselves.

Table of Contents

Introduction

No one walks down the wedding aisle hoping her marriage will dissolve into a divorce statistic. On our wedding day, we're full of hope and joy, and certainly a little stress from the preparations. We trust that this person we're joining with will be faithful and deserving of our love. We hope our values and goals will be somewhat the same as we age, even if we don't always see eye to eye. And we hope our communication will be strong enough to carry us through the bad times.

But what are we basing that on, really? When we marry young, say under 35 years of age, we're basing it on our dating history. Do we enjoy one another? Do we laugh together? Do we like the same sports? Do we have similar values around money, spirituality, and family?

The truth is we can't, with 100% surety, *know* any of that because people change and grow every day. Living is about change and growth. Hopefully, as a couple, we're changing and growing on paths that are near enough to overlap. As we age, our values seem to beckon us ever more deeply to express ourselves and our essence. Over time, it may take more work to help these paths cross over each other. At some mid-point in life, self-reckoning occurs for many.

Should I Stay or Should I Go Now?

I've seen dozens of couples who, upon this stage of self-reflection, began to realize their marriage was over. Some even realized it had been over for a period of years, yet they were still living together like old friends and roommates—but without a passionate dialogue between them on issues close to their hearts. You can imagine their sex lives weren't quite passionate either. Living together had become de rigueur, as if they were standing in the front yard and taking down the white picket fence one post at a time. With each post that comes down, you can hear them asking, "How long will the fence continue to stand? And what's really left?"

Some people spend years talking around the real issue. They talk about getting divorced and contemplate whether this is really the right choice for them, but don't take action. They tell their friends just a little about what's happening in their couples' counseling sessions. After all, they're making an effort to work on things. And it's truly worth a few years of working on your marriage before making such an important decision that has huge consequences.

Now, I know very well that all relationships wax and wane like a strong sturdy ship withstanding rough seas and calm waters. When we marry, we're hoping to upgrade from dinghy dating status to a smooth sailboat and then again to a weathered but sturdy cruiser. But for many, the particular waves that hit the marital ship are stronger than the vessel. How do we know when to jump ship, especially when the crew has grown to be more than the initial two?

I get so many people calling my office and wanting to talk about this one thing: ***How do I know my marriage is really over?*** I've compiled a list of questions to help you through this phase. Take your time answering them as honestly as possible.

Is My Marriage Really Over?

YES ☐ NO ☐

Is there a chance my marriage can be saved?

Divorce is a last resort. Although divorce is abundant in our culture, before taking that step, it serves you to be absolutely, 100%, without a doubt clear that there's NO chance you can reconciliate with your partner and live a fulfilling life. If there's even the slightest chance your marriage can be saved, congratulations! You have some work to do, and it can be profoundly gratifying.

YES ☐ NO ☐

Have I done everything possible to save my marriage?

Precisely because divorce is such a big part of our culture, this question is crucial. So I'll repeat it here. ***Have I done everything humanly possible*** *to save my marriage?* Am I being a loving partner? Am I listening to my partner's needs? Am I willing to engage with my partner about what's lacking in the relationship? And if so, are we making changes? Am I listening to *my* needs and most importantly sharing them? Am I expecting my partner to fulfill me when I'm not taking steps to fulfill myself?

YES ☐ NO ☐

Have we sought the advice of a minister, a trusted advisor, counselor, or friend?

Have I asked my partner to seek help with me regarding our relationship? Often it's helpful to get a third, objective point of view from someone who can provide guidance. Optimally, this is someone you both feel comfortable with. Conversations from this place can be highly useful and engaging.

YES ☐ NO ☐

Have I cried so many tears that I can't imagine crying any more over the sad state of my marriage?

It's not uncommon to grieve the marriage while you're still in it. This can take the form of depression with many tears or a paralysis of decision-making. We can distract ourselves for years to keep the pain of an unhappy marriage at bay. What I'm talking about here is a deep knowing that you're in the wrong marriage and distracting yourself by staying busy so you don't have to deal with the pain of losing the marriage. Sometimes this looks like a workaholic lifestyle or the super busy soccer mom. People stay together longer than warranted for many reasons. Jobs change, children grow, and extended families really do want the best for us. However, if you've been depressed and crying over your marriage for more than two years, it may be time to take inventory and see where you could shift an internal belief system about yourself or let go.

YES ☐ NO ☐

Have I forgiven my spouse for past hurts?

Resentments and bitterness can build up. The best path to mend them is through forgiveness. Have I forgiven myself for my role in what's not working? Am I expecting too much from my partner? This is a needed step whether or not you divorce. Respect the power of forgiveness.

YES ☐ NO ☐

Have I done my best to communicate my needs in the relationship in a way they can be heard?

When emotional intimacy is lacking, other parts of your marriage can go by the wayside too, like good sex and trust in your partner. Being willing to speak out about your needs can go a long way toward bridging the gap. Apologizing when you've not been at your best is a sign of maturity, not weakness.

YES ☐ NO ☐

Is there abuse in the relationship, whether physical, emotional, or substance?

If there is, that pretty much says it all. No one should stand for abuse. If you're unclear whether or not you're being emotionally abused, it's time to get clear about that. If you're justifying that it's only some of the time and mostly things are good, you may want to examine that as well. Why will it change? Could it get worse? And if there's substance abuse, are you willing to live with this long term?

YES ☐ NO ☐

Have I taken time away by myself to contemplate my choice?

Sometimes, we can go through a litany of checklists and read a ton of books when the truth, our truth, is available to us in each moment. For some people the truth is: It's too late to work on the relationship. Perhaps you've been trying for years and not getting anywhere with your partner. You can change you. You can't change your partner.

YES ☐ NO ☐

Have I made a list of the pros and cons of a divorce?

Lists can be helpful. Have you made a list, and if so, which side is weighted more heavily?

YES ☐ NO ☐

If I've checked off YES more than NO, have I looked ahead at what my life would be like without my partner?

It's important to gather your courage and be ready for the change if that's your choice. How you move into your next phase of life will have a lot to do with how happy you are in the long run as a single person or single parent. There's no ambivalence anymore when a marriage ends. Often that ambivalent state satisfied enough needs for you to stay. Are you prepared emotionally to leave? Do you have enough resources available to you to move on? What can you do if you don't? Do you have a support system in place?

How you work out these issues isn't done in a law office. If you're feeling anxious over all the decisions that need to be made, you're not alone. It's time to reach out for support from those who've walked the path before you. Take stock of your answers to the previous questions to determine your next step. You may want to meet with a professional, such as a divorce coach, to help you make your final decision.

When all the answers point toward divorce, or your spouse makes the choice for you, like many other couples, you might start with a separation. What better way to get some space and find what's true for you? Yet, even venturing into the sea of separation can be an anxious time. However, the fertile ground of new possibility is alive when someone takes a stand and says something has to change. Separation can be a vulnerable time, because as human beings, when we change, we typically change with apprehension and doubt, not sure if the change will be lasting or stick. If our marriage can't grow and change with us, it may feel like we're outgrowing the original marriage contract that held our hope.

Divorce Statistics

Contrary to popular belief, the divorce rate is not 50%. According to reporter Dan Hurley, this figure is misleading. He claims researchers say that the people divorcing in any given year are not the same as those who are marrying, so the annual statistic is virtually useless in understanding divorce rates. In fact, studies have found that the US divorce rate has never reached one in every two marriages, and with rates now declining, it probably never will. Additionally, about 60% of all marriages that eventually end in divorce do so within the first 10 years. And all experts agree that after more than a century of rising divorce rates in the US, the rates abruptly stopped going up around 1980.

The divorce rate per thousand people actually peaked in 1981 and has been declining over the ensuing quarter century. The divorce rate in 2005—3.6 divorces per thousand people—was at its lowest level since 1970. The number of people entering marriage as a proportion of the population in the US has also been falling for the past 25 years, and the marriage rate is currently at its lowest point in recorded history. The family is not a static institution.

History of Marriage

Here in America we romanticize love and marriage constantly. How did we come to a place where consistent, brilliant, stimulating conversation is consistently expected in a marriage? We've all heard that we can't expect our partner to "be everything to us", but how many of us expect that anyway, unconsciously?

Have you ever wondered how marriage began? The best available evidence I could find suggests that the institution of marriage began over 4,000 years ago. For thousands of years before that, anthropologists have surmised that families consisted of somewhat organized groups of around 30 people, with several male leaders, multiple women shared by them, and various children. As hunter-gatherers settled down into agrarian civilizations, the need for more stable arrangements seemed to arise. The first record of a marriage ceremony uniting a man and woman was around 2350 B.C. in Mesopotamia. For the next hundred years or so, marriage evolved into a more accepted institution for the ancient Hebrews, Romans, and Greeks. At that time, though, marriage had little to do with religion or love.

What was it about? The primary purpose of marriage initially was for the man's benefit—to bind women to men guaranteeing that a man's children were his true biological heirs. Through marriage, the woman became the man's sole property. In the ceremonies of ancient Greece, the father of the bride would turn his daughter over to the groom saying, "I pledge my daughter for the purpose of producing legitimate offspring." The ancient Hebrew men were free to take several wives, while the Greeks and Romans were free to satisfy their sexual urges with concubines, prostitutes, and even teenage male lovers. All the while, their wives had to stay home and take care of the household. If they didn't produce children, their mates could give them back and marry a different women.

When did religion become involved? When the Roman Catholic Church became powerful in Europe, a priest's blessing was necessary for a legal marriage. By the 8th century, the Catholic church accepted marriage as a sacrament or a ceremony upon which to bestow God's grace.

Did this change the nature of marriage? Church blessings improved wives' situations to some degree. Husbands were told to show more respect for their wives and weren't allowed to divorce them. Christian doctrine gave the husband and wife exclusive access to each other's bodies which put pressure on men to remain sexually faithful. But the church still supported men as the head of family, with wives deferring to their husband's wishes.

When did love enter the picture? A lot later than I would have imagined. Most of the marriages in the past brought men and women together for practical purposes, not because they fell in love. Over time though, many husbands and wives began to develop feelings of mutual love and devotion. But the idea of romantic love as the reason to marry goes back to around the Middle Ages. Historians think it started with the knight Sir Lancelot who fell in love with King Arthur's wife, Queen Guinevere. Twelfth-century literature reveals that men were advised to woo the object of their desire by complimenting her hair, eyes, and lips.

Did love change marriage? According to Marilyn Yalom, Stanford historian and author of *A History of the Wife*, the concept of romantic love began when women were permitted greater leverage in what had previously been a practical arrangement. The wife's purpose was no longer solely to serve her man. The romantic prince was committed to serve the woman he loved. Still, the notion that the husband "owned" his wife held on for a few more centuries. When colonists first landed on American soil, polygamy was still accepted in many areas of the world. The bride had to give up her name to symbolize surrendering her identity, and the husband was more significant, serving as the official public representative of two people, not one. Marriage rules were pretty stringent—any American woman who married a foreign-born man lost her citizenship.

How did this tradition change? In 1920, when women won the right to vote, the institution of marriage entered a dramatic transformation. Now, each marriage was for two full citizens, even though the tradition of the husband ruling the home still persisted. By the late 1960s, however, state laws that forbid interracial marriage were gone, and the last states had dropped any lingering laws against the use of birth control methods. By the 1970s, laws were in place that recognized marital rape, which until then was unheard of since the husband "owned" his wife's sexuality. "The idea that marriage is a private relationship for the fulfillment of two individuals is really very new," says historian Stephanie Coontz, author of *The Way We Never Were: American Families and the Nostalgia Trap.* "Within the past 40 years, marriage has changed more than in the last 5,000."

Where Do We Go From Here?

Marriage has indeed changed in the last 40 years, and divorce is one of the major changes. Marrying later in life is another. For some clients who married in their late 20s to early 30s, so much has changed. As one client, Gail, told me, "How could we have truly known ourselves to the point that we would stay with one mate, anyway?" How many of those who married at that time in their life did so because the marriage was a distraction from hearing the call of their purpose in life? Let's face it, it takes guts to do the hard thing and live the life you're called to.

And what are you called to do? If you're climbing Maslow's hierarchy of needs, once you have your physiological and safety needs met, you strive to climb higher to self-actualization. However, divorce can take you back down that ladder. It takes a great deal of trust to step down, believing that a few years of descending the ladder will bring you higher in the end. We all know how divorce exacts a heavy toll on finances and family life. The task then is to be willing to use divorce as a springboard to a better life. The fear inherent in deciding to divorce is about exactly THAT question: *Will I really be better off?*

Maslow's Hierarchy of Needs

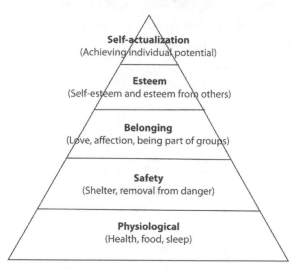

Self-actualization
(Achieving individual potential)

Esteem
(Self-esteem and esteem from others)

Belonging
(Love, affection, being part of groups)

Safety
(Shelter, removal from danger)

Physiological
(Health, food, sleep)

Once you're in the realm of divorce, you'll likely begin to notice others' thoughts and feelings on divorce. Obviously it's not your responsibility to take on their feelings, but many will offer plenty of advice. If you know you're someone who loves to be liked by others, your social life may rapidly change, as was the case for Tess. "I found I had to pull way in. I felt like I went through a two- to three-year period of not wanting to relate to other people until I had this primary relationship thing figured out. I stopped having parties. I stopped calling people to go to coffee and get together. I went through a period of uncertainty about the future, because I wasn't sure of myself. I didn't want to have to explain things to others. I knew that for me, I needed to trust myself and have my decisions be *mine*."

For another client, Barbara, there was the initial shock of not being supported by her community. For months after it became common news that Barbara was getting a divorce, one woman acquaintance at her church couldn't even look at her or say good morning as she had been doing weekly. It was as if this Christian woman no longer wanted Barbara in her reality. It took that woman literally six months before she could venture to say hello to Barbara again. And even then, it was her husband who spoke to Barbara first. Barbara felt judged and hurt, all while she was dealing with the sheer exhaustion from making difficult decisions and dealing with the ever-present grief that goes along with separation and divorce. Waking up daily with a grieving heart that trusts it's moving in the right direction through loss is like living in a thick fog, not really able to see what's ahead.

How we think and feel about separation and divorce has a lot to do with what the media has given us. How many times have we seen the advertisement for the mini van with 2.5 kids and a dog piling in? The next time you're out shopping, recognize that for every four mini vans you see, two of them are most likely carrying blended families.

Another client found that when she was able to overcome her fear of talking about living in a blended family, others followed suit. People she'd known in her business life fessed up that they too had been affected by divorce. She began to hear story after story of adults she now knew whose parents had divorced. Yet no one was talking about it openly. And of course, when we do the math, it makes perfect sense.

We've got years of programming in our brain and bodies that have held tightly to every syllable and whisper when people talk about divorce. Here are just a few phrases you might hear at a cocktail party or on the soccer field. If you don't hear them, trust that someone is probably thinking them.

- I can't believe she broke up her family. I would never do that.
- Those poor children.
- What will she live on?
- My marriage will never fail like that. *I* won't let it. Too bad *she* did.

If you're going through a divorce, believing these lines is like going down the rabbit hole. At times you may feel as crazy as Johnny Depp playing the Mad Hatter in the movie *Alice in Wonderland*. If you didn't "choose" your divorce, using it as a platform to further your growth is a great reward. The trap lies in being able to make the jump to willingly growing versus staying put in the misery of not having chosen this path. In the aftermath of divorce, you'll have many tough questions. Where do you find answers, especially when you're dealing with emotional turmoil, stress, and grief?

This book is about helping you answer these questions. My hope is to help you find certainty in your answers so you can move on with your life in a way that feels authentic and joyful. If you're divorcing, my desire is to inspire you to divorce well, in a way that has meaning for you.

We all know the grim statistics. Something has to shift for our children to have a brighter future with their friends and families. My own divorce story is one of survival, with lots of tears and laughter along the way. Modeling positive relationships for my daughter means a lot to me. That includes my co-parenting relationship with her dad. I'm so passionate about healthy relationships that I can feel it in my bones. It's what makes me *leap* out of bed in the morning instead of just placing my feet on the floor! I'm creating that shift for my daughter and myself. I hope you're inspired to do the same.

What is the Alchemy of Divorce?

The origins of Western alchemy are traceable to Egypt. Babylonian, Greek, Indian, and Chinese philosophers held that the complexity of nature can be explained with a small set of elements: Earth, Fire, Water, and Air. Alchemy then became the science of understanding, deconstructing, and reconstructing matter.

A common belief is that early alchemists' goals were to transmute common metals like lead into rarer ones like gold. This type of alchemy was highly documented, which led to a desire to make an elixir that would cure disease, making humans immortal—Inner Alchemy. In the Middle Ages, Persian and European alchemists put great effort into the search for this elixir. Pope John XXII issued a ban against alchemical counterfeiting, and the practice was banned in some circles.

Even in the 16th century, alchemy was a serious science in Europe. Isaac Newton studied and wrote more on alchemy than he did on the optics of physics, which he became known for. During the 17th century, practical alchemy began to evolve into "chemistry". Alchemists contributed to modern day trades such as metalworking and the making of ink, dyes, paints, and cosmetics.

Alchemical symbolism has been used by various psychologists. Carl

Jung looked at alchemical symbolism extensively and drew parallels to show the inner meaning of alchemical work as a spiritual path. The practice of alchemy was believed to change the mind and spirit of the alchemist.

For many women I've spoken with, there's a transformation that happens as we walk the path of divorce. One of the biggest changes occurs in our long held beliefs. Alchemy is this transformation that's at work, uncovering our desires and changing our internal beliefs. It's not a linear transition, and often we don't understand where we are in the process. We experience times of deep darkness and pain that bring us into the light of truth again—but only by walking through. Let me be your guide on your journey through the alchemy of divorce.

Keeping the Hope Alive

I've included a section of exercises at the end of each chapter titled **Keeping the Hope Alive**. The purpose of these exercises is to walk you through your current set of beliefs and discover what you're ready to shift and change for yourself. By completing these exercises, you'll be empowered during your divorce and have the ability to create the life you desire.

I've divided the exercises into three categories: **Bronze**, **Silver**, and **Gold**. After you do the exercises, repeat the affirmations, especially whenever you start doubting yourself and your decisions. Come back to the exercises in each chapter over time, moving up the levels as you're ready to claim your gold!

Level 1 Bronze

These exercises give you a starting point to traverse the maze of your divorce. Doing these is the bare minimum to complete your divorce fully intact. If you have children, you'll still need to sock away funds for their future counseling sessions.

Level 2 Silver

Kudos! You're on your way to clearing the emotional blocks that will likely occur during your divorce. Don't expect however, that all the crap between you and your ex will instantaneously be wiped away.

Level 3 Gold

Congratulations! You're going for the Gold! You're willing to invest more time and energy toward having a true divorce without drama. You understand that when you divorce well, it will have a huge positive impact on the future health of you and your family.

By working on your inner life, you'll strengthen your inner will. This will help you weather the dark days of your divorce. You'll feel stronger and have the resolve and faith you need to stand for yourself during your divorce process. Here's to you and your success!

CHAPTER 1

Surrendering to the Fire
How Am I Going to Get Through?

When two people decide to get a divorce, it isn't a sign that they "don't understand" one another, but a sign that they have, at last, begun to.
~ H. Rowland (English-American writer, 1876-1950)

Dear Abby,

I'm so lonely. My husband refuses to communicate with me or do anything with me. The only outlet I have is work and school. I would like to end this misery, but I don't know where to begin. We've been married for 17 years. I've never been unfaithful to him, although I have thought about it—not for the physical aspect, but for the communication.
Signed,
Desperate for someone to talk to

Dear Desperate:

Has your marriage always been this way? When did this "great silence" begin? Why have you tolerated an emotional "starvation diet"? If you think your marriage is worth saving, offer your husband the chance to repair it through marriage counseling. If not, formalize the reality that you haven't really been married in a very long time.

This is the place where you can face the facts: you're getting divorced even if you don't want to. You'll have lots of company, some who wanted their divorce and others who didn't. Well, no one really wants to get divorced, even those who "choose it" and make it happen. If your pending divorce has been held at bay, I bet you're already pretty tired. And yet you're going to need your strength and courage to make it through.

My client Emily came straight to my office shortly after her husband confessed his infidelity, and claiming not to love her anymore, he left her. Emily is a 43-year-old woman with three kids. She married Jack when she was 26. She's a wreck most days now. She cries her eyes out constantly, and who wouldn't? She's in terrible pain and barely holding things together. And she never even saw it coming. She's getting a divorce even though:

- ✓ She didn't want it.
- ✓ Her standard of living will drop.
- ✓ She never wanted her family to "fall apart".
- ✓ She tried hard to believe in and live "happily ever after".

Emily is at one of the most difficult stages of divorce. In time, she'll be able to lift her head off her morning pillow without totally cringing at daylight. But for now, she's sought help from her friends to get the kids to school so she can rest and create a plan for herself, all while deeply grieving.

Emily's path to divorce is in stark contrast to others' paths. Stephanie came into my office four years after her divorce had begun. She was still sweeping out old emotional patterns in order to create a new, loving relationship for herself. Unlike Emily, Stephanie was the one who filed for divorce. She shared with me the plan she'd made to prepare for her divorce.

"I knew two years before I filed that I wouldn't stay married to this man forever. Everything you hear about divorce and women involves how financially devastating it is for the woman. I was determined to not be one of 'those' women. So I made a plan. The first thing I did was get a post office box. This way, I could divert my personal bills and mail. Next, I got my own checking account at a separate bank. It was really more of a savings account. I purposely didn't get an interest bearing checking account so I wouldn't have to report interest income on our taxes. My paycheck varied from week to week, so the money I stashed was never missed. My husband never missed the mail, because life was all about him.

"The third thing I did was to get a storage unit. For me, this was a key factor. First of all, I began moving stuff out of the house. It's amazing how much stuff you can pack up and never miss. Second, when things were on sale, I bought them and stored them. This way I could let him have everything and there would be no arguments, no grounds for petty bickering. Why keep the old crap? I had all new stuff in my storage unit—linens, dishes, pots and pans, utensils, even cleaning products. Buy a little bit here and a little bit there and it all adds up over time.

"The hardest part for me was dealing with his anger. The bottom line was he was really hurt. Being as self-absorbed as he was, he never saw it coming. My biggest lesson from this was that the one who files for the divorce is willing to give up more than the other one."

Emily and Stephanie obviously had different paths to divorce. They are however, each on the same playing board. Once on the path, even though you may resist, it's time to let go and surrender. Surrender to living outside the box. So much will be changing: your finances, your home, your kids, your role as a partner, your new single status, and more. You'll now have to make a lot of decisions on your own. Gratefully, you don't have to do everything ALL alone! There are plenty of people with divorce experience who are farther along the path than you and are able to provide support.

Questions You Ask Yourself

It can be truly grueling to face getting divorced. So many questions go through your mind, such as:

How can this relationship be over?
What could I have done differently?
Have I really done everything I could to save it?

Why can't he work harder at this?
How come he couldn't tell me he was unhappy earlier?
Did he give me signs he was unhappy?

Is it okay to give up?
Will I be okay?
What will become of me and my children?

Why am I in this position when it's the last thing I wanted?
Will my family stand beside me with compassionate understanding?
Will my friends stand beside me?

Do I need a lawyer?
What is collaborative law?
How much does that cost?

Has he been charging high-ticket items on the credit cards?
Will he be better off financially than I am?
How will I financially prepare for my retirement?

How much will health insurance cost me now?
Will I be able to afford the same hairdresser?
Will I be able to afford the kids' extracurricular activities?

How much will my lifestyle suffer?
Which car will I end up with?
Can I afford to keep the house?

What will I do for work after staying home with the kids for so long?
Is he going to want more than half of the kids' time?
Will he even want to see the kids at all?

How will we handle the holidays?
Will he speak poorly of me to the kids?
Will the kids turn on me?

How will we split the kids' toys?
Will I forever be driving stuff around town?
Will he help them with their homework?

How will I cope with time on my hands when the kids are with him?
Will his new girlfriend try to be their mom?
Who will keep the dog?

What will the neighbors think?
What will it be like to be single again?
Who do I even know who's single?

Will I ever feel ready to date again?
Am I doomed to a life of Saturday nights with Netflix?
What if I dry up like a prune?

Will I ever stop crying?
How come I feel numb instead of angry?
How will my heart ever heal?

Will I ever feel normal again?
How will I handle the stress?
If there's a God, why doesn't he/she soothe my pain?

Why did we wait so long to get divorced?

Okay, now breathe. Slowly inhale, slowly exhale.

Sorry, that's a lot of questions. Maybe you've thought of some of these and not others. Take this time to sort out your feelings now.

Your Thoughts and Feelings

1. Right now what I'm feeling is:
   a. This sucks.   [   ]
   b. I'm not ready for this.   [   ]
   c. I'll somehow be okay.   [   ]
   d. _____

2. I can't believe he:
   a. Walked out.   [   ]

    b. Had an affair.   [   ]

    c. Doesn't love me.   [   ]

    d. _____

3. I'm ready to:

    a. Pull my hair out.   [   ]

    b. Move to Hawaii.   [   ]

    c. Hire a hit man.   [   ]

    d. _____

4. I don't have time for this because:

    a. The kids need me to _____

    b. My parents need me to _____

    c. I have to work.   [   ]

    d. _____

5. I know I need help but:

    a. Who can I trust? _____

    b. Who will listen? _____

    c. Who will really understand? _____

6. I'm most afraid of:

    a. Being alone.   [   ]

    b. Being broke.   [   ]

    c. Both a & b.   [   ]

7. Some of the more pressing questions I have are:

_____

_____

_____

8. Decide what your three next steps are and write them here:

    1. _____

    2. _____

    3. _____

Take control over what you can, which is yourself and your responses—**your response to life, to others, to yourself, and to your children.** Of course you're angry, tired, grieving, worn out, perhaps unstable, exhausted, spent, pissed, and so on.

Creating Supportive Structure

Separating two lives that have been entangled is challenging. So be gentle with yourself and create strategies to help you through. It's useful to create daily rituals that blend what *was*, with what's *needed now*. It's the simple rituals of life that keep us grounded and present to ourselves in the now.

For Anna, a single mom who wanted her divorce, a grounding ritual came in an unexpected form. "Two years after the divorce started, I found that the one thing that hasn't changed is I still love my morning coffee ritual. Every morning no matter what, I brew French Roast and sit in the same chair where I love the view. For me, a robust cup of java with my favorite creamer helps me feel ready to deal with anything from lawyers, to the ex, to whining children."

To keep from falling prey to the ever-present stress of divorce, create structures that help you breathe life into the day. Structure is a funny thing. For some people, the more structure they create, the better they feel. It provides a form to sink into, like a formula where feeling grounded and confident are the prize.

Here are some ideas that came forth during a support group:

1. Take a nightly bath. Light a candle and use bubbles. If wine sounds good to you, have a glass! Think only of the now.

2. Take a two-day stay-cation once every quarter. Unplug the phone and take care of yourself. Paint your nails, watch movies, and eat healthy! Do simple gardening or sleep in and read a novel.

3. Exercise at the same time every day in a way that nourishes you. For some, that may be walking outdoors alone. For others, it may be having a walking partner who holds you accountable. Others might want to swim three days a week and walk or run three days, with a day of rest. Make your schedule and stick to it.

4. Find community that's supportive, whether it's with one person or a group. Plan regular gatherings or outings. What's important is that it's reliable and a place where you feel you can truly share.

5. Do something simple with your girlfriends or children at the same time each week. Go to the park and swing. Find a creek to visit weekly, dipping your toes in during the summer months.

Slowly, the pain of your divorce will subside. As you pull yourself into each new day, be gentle and kind with yourself, even when you're having difficult moments. Remember that whatever you're feeling—be it numb, grief, or relief—you're not alone.

Keeping the Hope Alive

For each level, journal about the following:

Bronze

Make a list of 10 things you're grateful for having control over now, even if it's something as simple as "I can brush my teeth daily". Commit to one of the action items from the list of creating supportive structures or come up with your own. Tell a friend when you'll have that completed.

Silver

Journal about what new structure(s) you can put in place for yourself that will be supportive for you during this transition. Commit to one of them, as well as committing to two of the action items from the list of creating supportive structures. Find someone to hold you accountable to these items.

Gold

Start a gratitude journal where you list five things every night you're grateful for. Commit to three action items from the list of creating supportive structures. Find someone to hold you accountable to these items.

Affirmations

Repeat these whenever you start doubting yourself and your decisions.

I am good enough, right here, right now.
I am good enough, in every way.

CHAPTER 2

Painting Your Mask
From Victim to Heroine

It takes courage to grow up and become who you really are.
~e. e. cummings

Suffice it to say, divorce is a part of our collective landscape, therefore we owe it to ourselves to know how to do it well. It's only been in the last 50 years that women have been able to carve out financial stability to sustain a living on their own. This has given more women courage to make choices that truly are in their best interest.

Looking back on your life, this period of divorce may turn out to be a small blip. Or it may be the biggest change ever, where you finally claim all your power and know who you are. Yet, when you're in the divorce, it pays to know how to get through it with your sanity intact. This is sometimes difficult given the many worries we spin in our conscious mind.

A client, Joan, expressed that she was afraid of how her divorce would turn out. She was worried about her financial future and taking care of her children. At the same time she was deeply exhausted from trying to keep her family life together. She was terribly afraid of what the in-laws would think when they inevitably found out she was divorcing their son.

And she's not alone. In fact, I was married for 13 years even though it was over before that. I know how it feels to be in your shoes. I've endured the fear involved in ending a marriage—the heartache and the struggle of indecision.

I know what it feels like to be in a marriage that truly no longer fits who I am. For me, this came about through a spiritual calling. As I opened more and more to having God in my life, the cracks in my marriage became wider. I tried everything to move our marriage into a loving relationship, and it just wasn't happening.

It finally dawned on me that I wasn't being true to myself as a woman, that I had let my voice go unheard. I knew, without a doubt, I wasn't being the best role model I could be for my daughter. I was making myself miserable by staying in the marriage. I just couldn't do it anymore.

Now, I won't lie to you. It wasn't easy divorcing. It wasn't easy separating, moving out, dealing with child drop-off and pick-up. It certainly wasn't easy to contact lawyers and find the right one. But I persevered and learned so much along the way, while keeping my sanity! I literally changed the course of my future through my divorce.

Maybe you can relate to my story or Joan's. Whether or not you're choosing divorce, how much of yourself have you put on the shelf to keep your marriage going?

For women, a major component of how well they do after divorce has to do with how they moved into the divorce. Simply put, either they saw and felt the divorce coming, or they didn't. The more conscious and willing a woman is to see the end of the relationship, the easier it is to accept. This doesn't lessen the grief, but it does smooth the process of moving on.

Victims

Some women who consult with me say they had no idea their husband was so unhappy and ready to leave the marriage. For these women, it comes as a hard truth that they now have to be conscious to what was unconscious before. Most of them go into some type of shock and block off their emotions just to cope. They often feel as if their world has totally collapsed and they're left adrift.

For many of these women, there's a persistent nagging question: "If I wasn't able to see the signs that the primary person I was committed to was so miserably unhappy, what else have I not been able or willing to see?" At times these women may want to pretend that really, truly this other person was happy, when that's not the case. At least it's not the case any longer.

Most of the women I've worked with have a deep distrust that they'll be "okay" after the divorce. They have the hardest time adjusting, and they tend to linger in their divorce healing. Some never grow into the heroine and stay the victim the rest of their lives. This may look like having to stay on a strict budget, or becoming bitter, or not having many friends. Often they never date or they don't enjoy dating, projecting their hatred of their ex onto all men. It can become a depression that lasts a lifetime. "If only" becomes their mantra.

When pressed hard, some of these women admit to simply ignoring the signals their husband had been giving that he *was unhappy*. Following are several lies victims may tell themselves:

- No, there wasn't any lipstick on his shirt.
- I'm sure he's actually playing poker or golf with his coworkers.
- He works really hard and *needs* to work late all the time.

- Of course all those texts are from his work buddies!
- Looking at the credit card bills won't tell me anything I don't already know.

It's entirely natural to have that "first married" feeling pass. It's not natural however to have no communication beyond "we're out of milk" in a marriage. There's a huge difference between managing the logistics of daily living and sharing intimate details in a relationship. Women need the sharing of feelings to create intimacy. A mature woman (heroine) changes her stance from "this is what a marriage is like and it sucks," to "something needs to change here".

For someone who isn't ready to make that shift in her thinking, she chooses to stay unconscious—a victim. She won't see signs of unhappiness. And she won't even look for them. If a woman can admit to the truth that she wasn't seeing and listening to signals that her man was unhappy, she's ahead in the ball game of relationship success. She can then become conscious of her own power in the situation. Yes, there is grieving to be done and mistakes to be forgiven, but she'll be able to transcend these into a full life for herself.

Heroines

In my office, I see many women who wanted their divorce. Often they gave up on any effective communication with their spouse or realized their marriage wasn't going to weather the changes they needed. These women are often quite attuned to their emotional selves and their needs. Some are full time working moms. They're already fairly independent. They describe a situation where they felt they grew emotionally and spiritually and began to want more from the relationship than what was there. Sometimes, people simply wake up to a part of themselves they haven't paid attention to before.

It's not that their values change, but their priorities do. After all, that's what growth is about—changing priorities. No one's really at fault. In this case the two people don't mesh anymore—someone just outgrew the other. And when a relationship can't grow and change anymore, a split occurs.

Many people live in a relationship for years where there's a split, while others choose to take the next step by divorcing. When my client Cecilia was asked what the last straw was that broke the camel's back for her, she said, "I literally felt like I was dying from the inside out. I knew if I stayed, I didn't have a chance to be truly happy. In the end, I had to make the move to save myself."

The women who choose to divorce have an easier time moving on. Heroines consciously choose to look at how they were responsible for each piece of their marriage, including the pieces that weren't working. They become empowered by engaging in moving forward. This takes time and effort as they commit to practices that help them walk through the emotions and motions of divorce. They learn to strive toward new things in their life. They make new friends, create new work, and do whatever it takes to live life anew, without blaming the past.

Take a moment now to think about how you'll move forward with your divorce. Will you proceed as a victim, a heroine, or somewhere in between?

Let's begin by looking at five areas of divorce:

- ➤ Legal Issues
- ➤ Financial Independence
- ➤ Social Life
- ➤ Relationship with Children
- ➤ Blame

Legal Issues

Victim – She let's the ex take the lead to just "get it over with". She feels inundated by all requests for appointments, paperwork, schedule changes, etc.

Heroine – She deeply trusts the timing and the process. She goes slowly enough to make decisions powerfully, while educating herself and choosing the type of divorce best suited to her situation.

Financial Independence

Victim – She doesn't change her buying habits to reflect a possible change in circumstances. She sticks her head in the sand when it comes to budgeting or big financial decisions.

Heroine – She has the guts, stamina, and determination to stand up for what she deserves in the settlement. She creates a budget that she follows and adjusts as needed. She meets with her financial planner to stay informed.

Social Life

Victim – She sits alone frequently after work and on weekends. She buries herself in only doing activities centered around her children.

Heroine – She creates new friendships that truly serve her now. She checks out different social groups, persisting until she's made new friends with whom she connects. She seeks support for getting back into the dating world and dates confidently, when she's ready.

Relationship with Children

Victim – She pines for the kids when they're with her ex, and calls too frequently to speak with them, creating havoc. She fights with her ex in front of the children. If she has the children full time, she rarely hires a sitter so she doesn't have to be without them.

Heroine – She gets support for handling difficult emotions concerning wanting to control her children's time with her ex. If she has the children full time, she creates a large support network to bolster her family and provide positive role models.

Blame

Victim – She blames her ex for more than 50% of the problems in the marriage. She's unable to imagine a new life for herself, seeing each new day as dreary. She let's the divorce drag on and doesn't reach out for support.

Heroine – She finds creative outlets for her emotions when she feels like blaming her ex, knowing she's also responsible. She empowers herself by getting support to reflect on her past, accept her choices as her own, and claim her power in all facets of her life to move forward.

Because we're unique women, we may find ourselves a **victim** in one area and a **heroine** in another. If that's the case for you, focus on taking the energy from the areas where you *are* a heroine into the other arenas. Keep asking yourself: "What's the powerful move here?"

And remember that divorce doesn't solve everything:

- ➢ The sink still backs up
- ➢ The cat still sheds
- ➢ The car still needs gassing and washing
- ➢ The laundry is still never done
- ➢ The extra weight is still there
- ➢ Allergies still cause havoc
- ➢ Kids still need to be fed and loved
- ➢ Parenting is still taxing

Letting Go, Ever So Gently

Letting go is often a part of the picture in divorce. As my client Jill summed it up, "Unfortunately, this is a time when I'm letting go of my illusions of who I am and what I need to live or be comfortable. I've had to let go of so many clothes, accessories, and kitchen items since I moved. The moving actually helped me to pare down and recognize what's truly important. A soup tureen, probably not. Family photos, you bet. Keeping my daughter's art on the walls? Absolutely. They're a reminder to her that she matters, that I care for her.

"Do I miss the nice house? Yes, sometimes. And other times I'm gloriously happy that I no longer have to buy toilet tissue for three bathrooms. It all depends on how I choose to look at it. Downsizing for me has meant increased freedom. How much space do I truly need, anyway? What's the future of the planet if everyone lived in a 3,000 square foot home?"

Change is in the air—and chaos. That means sometimes you'll feel like you're on an emotional roller coaster and sometimes your children will too. In short, even though this may sound cruel, don't hang on to what you *no longer have*. Accept the facts, deal with the realities, handle your emotions, and move on. A divorce can be a long-term project where the project management gets messy and the deadlines are sure to be extended way beyond what anyone wanted. The first thing to do is recognize that fact and accept it as best you can.

Jill asks herself, "*Am I happier?* You bet! My life is based on my goals, desires, and needs. Even when I'm riding the roller coaster of co-parenting, I get to respond to the choices that need to be made. *Is there pain?* Absolutely! And I'd say more joy as well. Now I'm feeling alive. Before I lived in a fog of doubt, oppression, and mired choices, mixed with despair over how things were going to get better.

There's strength in letting go and accepting. This is the beauty of being a woman. We can hold so much pain and love all at the same time. Yet, it's really only in the letting go that we can move into acceptance of what is. That we can move on to the next stage a little bit stronger. When we can sit with the fullness of what is, we can open up and feel our compassionate heart."

> **A plant can't live without roots.**
> **Your soul is your root.**

Keeping the Hope Alive

For each level, answer the question and journal your thoughts.

Bronze

In terms of heroine consciousness, where are you on a scale of 1-10 in the following areas? Know that this can change over time.

Legal Issues

Circle the number that indicates where you are.

1. **Victim**: Feeling inundated by all requests.
5. **Awakening Woman**: Gets things done but procrastinates.
10. **Heroine**: Educates herself and asks for help.

1   2   3   4   5   6   7   8   9   10

Victim   Awakening Woman   Heroine

Financial Independence

Circle the number that indicates where you are.

1. **Victim**: Gonna party like hell.
5. **Awakening Woman**: Adopts "I'm okay for now" attitude.
10. **Heroine**: Sticks to her budget and supplements with new work if needed.

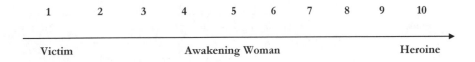

Social Life

Circle the number that indicates where you are.

1. **Victim**: Spends too much time alone.
5. **Awakening Woman**: Makes new acquaintances but doesn't call them for support.
10. **Heroine**: Dates when ready and is conscious of her boundaries.

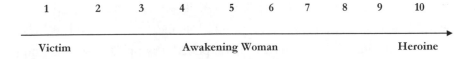

Relationship with Children

Circle the number that indicates where you are.

1. **Victim**: Allows parental alienation from husband.
5. **Awakening Woman**: Agrees to fair custody schedule but tries to control ex's relationship with children.
10. **Heroine**: Focuses on strong bonds with her children when she has them and creates supportive adult time for herself when children are with ex, letting them be.

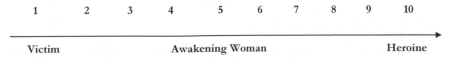

Blame

Circle the number that indicates where you are.

1. **Victim**: Frequently battles with ex in her head.
5. **Awakening Woman**: Journals the battles to release them.
10. **Heroine**: What battles? I'm creating my reality.

1	2	3	4	5	6	7	8	9	10

Victim   Awakening Woman   Heroine

Silver

Pick one area from the bronze level to create a shift in for yourself. Pick one of the easier categories to experience an accomplishment. Your goal is to feel empowered. What number would you like to bring this area to? What will you do to bring that number up?

Gold

Give yourself permission to imagine what it would be like to be a heroine in each of the categories: Legal Issues, Financial Independence, Social Life, Relationship with Children, and Blame. Journal what this feels like for yourself. Make it come to life on paper! Then pick two areas and write out action items that you commit to.

Affirmations

Repeat these whenever you start doubting yourself and your decisions.

> *I trust myself fully.*
> *I truly love myself.*

CHAPTER 3

Your Heart's Magic
7 Ideas for Cultivating Compassion in a Time of Grief

❧

The first divorce in the world may have been a tragedy,
but the hundred-millionth is not necessarily one.
~ Anatole Broyard, American literary critic

Now that you're clear you're in a divorce, and even though you may not like the idea of it, it's time to be gentle and compassionate with yourself. So many things are going on, to be sure. Through all of it, three areas need particular attention; your grief, your integrity, and your self-care. Here are some questions we'll look at in this chapter:

1. What does it mean to grieve?

2. What does it mean to divorce with integrity?

3. Why is it important to have the right support?

Grief

My client Emily is mortified to find herself in this position. She's slumped in her chair with her wrinkles and thinning hair. She'd loved him. How could he have done this to her? To their family? Everything they'd worked so hard for, now gone. Down the drain. His affair had ruined any speck of trust they might have had. Damn him anyway! Now he was going to make the kids' lives hell too. Their college funds soon to be eaten by the divorce lawyers, paying for *their* kids to go to college, not hers.

Too much to think about, Emily loads the washing machine one more time. Little does she realize that although the laundry is never done, something in her finds relief in the familiarity of the task. Soon the kids will be home and she'll be absorbed by them and won't even have time to think about her future.

But as the kids get ready for bed, she finds herself irritable with them, angry that soon she'll be alone with her thoughts and fears, instead of the way it used to be. Before, she held the illusion that things were fine behind her white picket fence. Truth is, she and John hadn't really shared their days or thoughts for some time. Typically, at the end of the day, he'd go into his home office and she'd do something in the kitchen or watch TV.

How long had it been since they'd even been somewhere without the kids? How long had he been seeing this other woman? Why hadn't she known? And to hear that she was so much younger. Her heart ached. Her eyes hurt from crying. That bitch! Didn't she know she was breaking up a family?

Today, her lawyer mentioned gently that she needed to think about going back to work. There wasn't going to be enough money to go around. But, she didn't want to think about that. She'd left her career years earlier to stay home with the kids. That's what they'd agreed on. She should stay home so the kids would be well taken care of and feel loved. She hadn't counted on him straying and wanting a divorce.

It's true, maybe she should have pushed harder for that date night once in a while, like her neighbor Patty had started doing with her husband. They seemed to be doing okay now, although one could never really know. Just like she hadn't known.

Divorce isn't something that's easily talked about in some circles. Says Barbara, "I was part of a women's group for over a year, and that whole time, not one of us brought up our marriages. Now that's a lot of pain being hidden under the table."

Many kinds of losses are involved in grieving a marriage. Unfortunately, at times it feels more complicated than grieving the loss of a parent or loved one, which is difficult enough. When we lose our marriage, we lose a variety of roles. We lose not only the role of wife and mate, but also of being a married person. Sometimes, we lose the role of full-time mom. Often as women, we lose the role of stay-at-home-mom too.

The key to coming out whole as a single person is to deal with the reality of being in a divorce—deal with the losses, one at a time. Grieve them. Feel them. Let the losses be felt and acknowledged. It's only in acknowledging a loss that something else will spring forth.

When I lost my father in '92, I made an altar that I prayed at daily in his honor. I didn't feel like making an altar to my marriage. I no longer wanted to stare at a picture of my soon-to-be-ex-husband. Don't be surprised if the grief of losing your mate feels different than other grief you may have experienced. For some people, losing their marriage may be their first experience with grief. In our culture, we've lost many rituals that honor the grieving process, yet they're so needed. They tie us to the reality that we'll live and laugh again. It's by working through the grief that we come to the other side and find something in ourselves that's ready to emerge fresh, never before seen.

In the sadness over the pain of losing our marriage, even hearing a certain song may bring us to tears. Shedding these tears is an important part of our recovery. Crying is one of the most common forms of letting go and it moves you into the compassionate heart. It allows you to feel again, where you might have been numbing yourself to your pain.

In my divorce coaching practice, I've met many people who've been separated for four years or more. And still, some of them haven't finished their divorce. They each have their reasons for not having completed their divorce and yet, as we dig deeper, invariably we find there's more grief they have yet to address. I'm the first to admit that dealing with loss takes time, and yet it's well worth the effort. Unresolved grief can lead to illness or just being stuck in a depressive rut!

When the tears come, let them. Somewhere I read that every time we cry we heal a piece of ourselves. Grief is like an ocean with waves of its own. We can't know when or where we'll feel its depths, but it's waiting there for us to shine healing light on. After a good cry, many people, myself included, feel lighter. Have patience with your grief, as it's truly an act of self-love. What I've noticed is the more patience I have with myself, the more I have with my child, and others. Be willing to let your patience grow.

We learn to come to grips with losing the illusion that all is well. Often due to financial concerns, we lose a beloved home and possibly even a pet. We may even lose a circle of friends who had kept us going and been a nice buffer between ourselves and our deluge of worries. It's still a common story for women to lose friendships with their married friends. We lose a lot. It's like a spiritual surrender, discovering what's really important. As author and workshop leader, Byron Katie says, "When you fight reality, you lose." To me that means when someone fights the inevitable—that they're IN a divorce—it's a losing fight. Let go, let go, let go…

Check out these valuable ways to deal with grief:

1. Journal your thoughts and feelings.
2. Go to a grief workshop or support group.
3. Set up an altar and take time to pray and connect to what's truly important.
4. Pour your feelings into a piece of art—a painting, sculpture, or drawing.
5. Take a hike alone and dedicate the time to your ending marriage.
6. Cry in a hot tub where the tears become part of something larger.
7. Pick one night a week to eat your favorite comfort foods.
8. Watch a tearjerker love story on TV.

Write your ideas here:

_____

_____

_____

Integrity

Just when we think we're doing well with letting go, integrity weighs in like a boulder headed downhill. What does it mean to you to divorce with integrity? And how can you stay in integrity through all the grief and anger? We feel better about ourselves when our choices are in line with our integrity. Our integrity is the set of principles that guide our choices now.

There will be life after divorce. The new people you'll be meeting will possibly be interacting with you and your ex, especially if you have children. So your future dates are going to know a thing or two (or three) about how you divorced. That means if you want to be part of a couple or marry again, pay attention to making wise choices now.

For my client Suzanne, having integrity during her divorce meant not being rude to her pending ex during drop-offs for her children, even though she felt *he* was rude. Having her children come out of the divorce as stable as possible was an important value for her. For others, having integrity may mean paying close attention to choices like:

- Am I choosing a fighting lawyer?
- Am I being respectful of my children's time with their dad?
- Am I speaking poorly of my ex in front of my children?
- Am I allowing others to speak poorly about my ex in front of my children?

Self Care is Supportive, Not Selfish

Many of us live with an ingrained myth that putting ourselves first is selfish. By deeply listening to our needs, I believe we can discern when it's important to put ourselves first and when to put others first. Certainly there are times for listening to and helping others. Yet there's also a time to take care of ourselves.

Truly taking care of ourselves can be spending time alone, scheduling time with friends, or picking up a new hobby. During your divorce, it may be to keep educating yourself by talking with others who've been through divorce. It's by deep listening that we'll know our next step.

As a newly single person, I find it daunting to keep all the balls juggling in the air. I have the roles I play and the things I do, which can overlap on any given day looking like a jungle gym. Most women know exactly what I mean. And yet, I'm so used to keeping all the balls in the air. For myself, as for other women I've spoken with, distracting oneself with projects becomes a way of coping with a difficult marriage while we are in it. This becomes so learned and ingrained that when we're on our own, the extra work of being single feels like only one small thing added to the list. We all know we're supposed to be saying "No" to new commitments, but how many of us really are?

Following is an example of a compilation of *my* list of juggled items. I share this with you so you can see you're not crazy yourself! See what you relate to in the following list:

Clean house
Put good food on the table for myself and kid
Be wise parent

Rotate tires
Floss teeth
Feed cat

Water garden
Clean out garage
Plant flowers

Buy new computer
Pay bills
Pick up lizard tails that cat brought in

Be happy
Do laundry
Call fridge repair guy

Pray
Get hug from Amma
Start new diet

Download iPod tunes
Learn to order at Starbucks
Find clothes that fit AND look good

Get rid of wrinkles
Find time to laugh
And something to laugh about

Grieve losses
Speak more clearly with ex
Gather camping gear

Wonder about new dating interest
Worry about daughter
Wish life were simpler

Complete 401k rollover
Find summer childcare
Train for marathon

Cry
Check calendar re period
Clean spots on carpet

Wish stepdad Happy Fathers Day
Eat more fruit
Find quality time with boyfriend

Clean out emails
Plan a play date for kid
Take a bath

Give in, knowing I can't hold it all
Breathe
Sigh

Time has a way of creeping up on us though. After several years of this overdriven type of behavior, we begin to see the toll it's taking on us. Illnesses may erupt to slow us down. One positive thing that can come from divorce for many women is that we finally learn to *really* take care of ourselves. We spend more time with exercise and warm baths. We take greater care to schedule time with friends who are truly supportive. This is a time when many women make a larger commitment to their spiritual path, whether that's through attending church or meditating regularly. Ironically, it takes a bit of work to know, in your bones, that self-care is not selfish. It takes making mistakes and re-setting boundaries time and again. But it's oh so worth the effort to reclaim each part of ourselves that's been calling us home.

Our hearts get injured after years of neglect and slogging through marriages that don't quite fulfill us. We become mired down and our soul gets weary. Rest, rest, rest, it whispers. On a good day we listen. I took a lot of time to rest after separating. At times I wondered if I'd ever feel the desire to truly move around and accomplish anything again. What I've come to see is that I moved quicker, as I was ready, as if from a springboard—precisely because I gave myself the space and time I needed to rest. I'll always have dishes, laundry, and gardening. For the modern woman, chop wood, carry water has become wash, dry, and fold laundry.

Take time away by yourself if you can. I found an amazing getaway on the coast of California called Costanoa. They offer little cabins and a hot tub. And the cabins have electric blankets on the beds! They also offer massage. I'd go there two to three times a year, as it's very affordable. I'd take my art supplies and my journal. Great hiking abounds with many trails available. And I could be with me, all of me—to reclaim the pieces that had been lurking in the background for too long. I typically went on a Wednesday through Friday so I was free to experience a quieter place with fewer couples. Not such a great idea to have your getaway time intruded upon by being faced with loving couples when you're aching from not having that very thing.

Creating a support system that works for you is invaluable. Possibilities are new single friends, a lawyer you see eye to eye with, a counselor, or a trusted friend. You can find meetup groups (www.meetup.com) and support groups everywhere these days. Putting this system in place is truly taking care of yourself.

Keeping the Hope Alive

No matter whether you choose divorce or divorce chooses you, grief is inevitable. It's a loss, and how you mourn that loss will affect how nimble you are in moving forward in your life after your divorce. It also affects how ready you are to move through your divorce and whether you make choices that are in integrity with your values.

Bronze

Answer the following questions by journaling.
- How am I prepared to deal with the grief of my loss?
- How is my relationship going with my ex?
- What do I need to change in myself to be in integrity?

Silver

Do you have a daily practice to handle your grief? If not, choose one that you'll commit to for one week. Suggestions are to journal daily, spend time in prayer, or create a grief collage.

Gold

Prepare an altar and include an object from your marriage that has great sentiment for you. Commit to spending 10 minutes a day for one month reflecting at your altar and acknowledging your grief. Write down a moment when you had to talk with your ex and you held yourself to your highest level of integrity. An example is: "We had to talk about selling the house and I didn't raise my voice like I have in the past."

Affirmations

I am here in the NOW.
I have patience with myself.

CHAPTER 4

Who's Stirring the Pot?
5 Excuses That Spoil the Soup of Separating Effectively

*If you made a list of reasons why any couple got married, and another
list of the reasons for their divorce, you'd have a lot of overlapping.*
~ Mignon McLaughlin, American Journalist and Author

Joanne recently came to my office after a friend referred her. Dressed in
the latest fashions and carrying a nice purse, I noticed when she spoke
that she wasn't feeling powerful at all. She was feeling trapped, like she
couldn't leave her husband. Here's a synopsis of excuses I've heard from
her and others:

1. There's no money to leave.
2. I'm afraid I'll be alone forever.
3. I'm afraid I'll have to go to work and I don't want to.
4. I'm afraid I'll become a bag lady.
5. I'm afraid my kids will suffer.
   Notice a pattern here?

We'll dissect each one of these further. Because, let's face it, our minds
can race with worry or we can get clear.

A few years ago, the sermon at my church was focused on relationships.
Now somehow, I'm sure it was tied to the Bible. But today, I can't tell you

how. What I heard was, "It's a sin to stay in a relationship for the lifestyle it affords you." Certainly too, it's a sin against oneself to stay in a relationship if there's abuse going on, whether physical or emotional. Sin here is defined as something not good for oneself, something that God, Goddess, or Spirit wouldn't want for you. Something not in your highest good.

After that particular service, my then-husband and I went to lunch with another family and all our children. Naturally, we discussed the sermon over Dim Sum. I found it ironic that my husband hadn't heard that part of the sermon at all. He was still fuming over some political issue between the Republicans and the Democrats. But the other three of us at the table had heard it loud and clear. If you know your marriage is over and you're staying for the lifestyle, it's time to move on. And if there's abuse going on, physical or emotional, it's time to move on as well. Of course, I'm assuming here that you've done all you can to rectify the situation. You've tried to bring the love back. You've sought help for the abuse issues. You've done your part to improve communication.

1. There's no money to leave.

It's far easier to split no money than to split millions of dollars, trust me. What people are expressing is the fear that they won't have money to rent a separate apartment, or buy groceries, or pay the gym membership so they can still look fabulous while single. Yes, lawyers can be expensive, but there are ways to keep the expense of divorce down. We'll get to the legal stuff in chapter 8.

The important thing here is rather than living in the fear of "what if", it's time to get into action and create a separate budget so you can see exactly how much you need and how it will be spent. Check out www.mint.com as many of my clients have to keep good track of your money.

2. I'm afraid I'll be alone forever.

What's worse? Being alone in a relationship or being fully alone? OK, well maybe being fully alone, but being alone in a relationship is definitely crazy making in the long term. Here's Brenda's story:

"I knew something was off with my marriage when I was sitting home alone on a Saturday night with my five-year-old child tucked safely in bed. A friend from work came over to get my signature on something. I was feeling smug about sitting around in my clean house while trying not to feel alone. But the way she responded told me something valuable. Her face went a bit slack as she recognized my loneliness. It gave me great insight. I was alone, there was just no denying it. I was living a lonely existence. My husband had left again on another trip. For some reason, he'd had to leave that Saturday. If it were an occasional thing, I could've lived with that, but when occasional becomes the norm, it hurts. I was hurting inside and I barely knew it. Here I was in our beautiful home, alone. It wasn't the first time I'd been left without him—after all he needed to travel 'to provide a roof'—and it wasn't the last time either."

Answer these two questions honestly:

What will my life be like in five years if we stay together?
And if we separate, what do I see for myself in five years?

When you've tried your best to reignite your love and it hasn't worked, you can transfer those skills into meeting new people. When you do that successfully, your life will be rich. There are lots of single people out there living full, rich, brilliant lives. Here's a short list of things you can do to meet people:

- Take a dance class
- Join a class at the gym
- Talk to people at your favorite coffee shop
- Join an online meetup group
- Take a class at adult school
- Socialize after religious/spiritual services
- Put up profiles at a dating site and social networking sites

3. I'm afraid I'll have to go to work and I secretly don't want to.

Part of becoming whole is using all of our talents. This means we get to be great moms, multi-tasking like crazy and bringing home money from our work. Taking off the full-time mom hat and putting on the hat of breadwinner is tough for many. In all my work, I honestly think it's the women who've stayed at home to take care of children who have the hardest time moving on. For those women who are already in the work force prior to divorcing, their identity has something to cling to: their work. They have a built-in social situation. They have structure in their day-to-day life.

For those of you who secretly don't want to go back to work, find something in it that's freeing—even if it's one idea you can live with. It can be totally humbling to find yourself behind the espresso machine over the age of 40. But if it's helping to pay the mortgage or get your child through college, it's a good thing. There can be solace in that alone.

Often I find half the battle of moving on is the shift of identity. It's such an identity shift to go from stay-at-home mom to working single mom. It's so much easier to keep pretending that clean rugs, a clean sink, and food in the fridge will make everything okay, rather than to surrender to a messy house and financial integrity by finding work! I used to distract myself from the pain in my marriage by focusing on cleaning and having a sparkling house. So for me, that's what I knew: clean, clean, clean. For others this might be exercise or reading books, especially escapist romance novels! Once divorced however, these patterns must change to be a fully, whole, functioning person. And believe me, these patterns of distraction will rear their heads.

What to do when that occurs? Hopefully you'll notice it for what it is…a distraction. Staying focused on the true, important tasks at hand takes deep effort at times, as well as gut-wrenching honesty. Looking back on my divorce, I wish I'd been more honest with myself about earning money to stop the drain of the bank account earlier.

4. I'm afraid I'll become a bag lady.

And for those who keep resisting working, the bag lady fears may keep you up at night. Believe me, I know! Never mind that we might not have money for Botox or that planned tummy tuck. Secretly, many of us are afraid we'll become the bag lady pushing the shopping cart across the intersection with our sleeping bag stuffed inside.

"I thought he would take care of me." Many women coming into my office echo this heart-breaking sentiment. The wise woman knows that no one else can truly take care of her needs. They just can't. Not really. Only you can truly take care of your deep, inner needs.

Unfortunately this desire to be taken care of can also spill over into the finances, especially for women who made the choice with their partners to stay home to care for children instead of remain in the work force. And to make matters worse, self-esteem can plummet by staying home, especially if your spouse doesn't value your role as primary caregiver.

Learning to stand on your own two feet, especially financially after losing someone you loved and trusted for so long, can be a rewarding challenge, or it can be a bitch. It's hard to turn off the care-giving roles we've become accustomed to: mothering, giving to neighbors, etc., and focus on profit-oriented tasks. For many women, getting a job really is a good answer. It's a place to learn that we're valued. And it can give us the time we need to recover from our grieving hearts and the financial toll of divorce.

When does the cry of "keeping the kids stable" become the crutch of co-dependency on them? There's a balancing line between wanting to be available to our children and acknowledging even for ourselves how the reality of our situation has changed. Young children require incredible amounts of love, attention, and care. Those who have family nearby to help with childcare are blessed. Many in this era, however, live far from other family, so, it's hard to get everyone's needs met.

The tough question is: at what point does barely paying the bills so you can keep picking your kids up from school become a hazard to everyone's long term well being? As in, how will we pay for college? And, what part of being a stay-at-home mom feeds in to the low self-esteem of not seeing oneself as a valuable player in the world market of making money? This can be a difficult area for many women going through divorce—to swallow that their standard of living has lowered and they now have to do whatever it takes to bring in more money. Talk to other women about how they got through this time, and asses your skills for entering the job market. There are many programs available to support people re-entering the workforce.

You have to put the fear aside one day at a time by focusing on what's right in front of you.

As Brenda found out, "Now I have other single parent friends who are really accepting and generous when I need help. I moved to a street we jokingly call 'divorce cul-de-sac'. Half the people here are going through a divorce and have children. My new friends are willing to talk to me about the realities of life. We have more community now. We know our neighbors, and they don't ask odd questions about our crazy schedule. There's a great deal of acceptance among our new friends—acceptance for the fact that we're dealing with a lot of hurt and making the best of it. There's no one here telling me I should try to work on saving my marriage when it wasn't salvageable."

5. I'm afraid my kids will suffer.

Hmmm. This is a tough one. Will your children's lives change? Yes. Will they change anyway? Yes. Will all your children's problems or issues be the result of your divorce? No. Will staying in an unhappy marriage affect your children? The answer to that plays a big part in how you look at leaving your marriage. If you believe you'll be better off, then I believe your children will too. Though, it may take time.

Creating a positive co-parenting relationship will take time. Do your best to see the silver lining. Suzanne's children ended up having a relationship with their dad after she had done all the early childhood caretaking. I hear story after story of parents who, prior to divorce, hadn't really been a part of their child's life. When faced with the divorce, they begin to step it up. Parents who up until now hadn't taken part in the day-to-day care of their child/ren, often begin to do more of that, which is wonderful for the children, even if it's confusing at first.

So exactly who holds the power? That's what we're talking about here. For many women, working through their divorce issues is about reclaiming their power. I've met with several women who are choosing to stay in their homes for "the sake of the kids". And although they're "technically" divorced, the financial settlements aren't finished until they can divide the house assets. Many of these same women have difficulty with their ex-husbands. They harbor fear about moving forward and finishing the financial piece and their ex's prey upon that, knowing they're afraid of losing the house before they're ready. Each of these women has to decide what's the most empowering stance they can take. Anger is the problem. Getting through is the answer.

Keeping the Hope Alive

Bronze

Journal about the roles you each played in your marriage. When it comes to money, were you traditional or untraditional? What would you have changed? If you haven't already, create a budget. How prepared are you for a positive financial future?

Silver

What are your current thoughts about money? Do you shy away from people with money? If so, why? What areas of your divorce (children, finances) do you still need to look at and decide what you will want, bottom line?

Gold

What/who do you believe is the true source of supply? What are you wanting to hold out for in the divorce and why? What can you make peace with that you may not get?

Affirmations

I firmly believe in my abilities.
I'm powerful and unstoppable!

Chapter 5

Transforming Your Closest Tribe
Three Relationships That Change

Make new friends but keep the old,
one is silver and the other's gold.
A circle is round it has no end,
that's how long I'm going to be your friend.

Oh, how I wish that simple song held more truth for me. My daughter used to sing that in Girl Scouts and as co-leader, I sang right along. That was before my divorce. By far one of the more devastating pieces of my divorce has been losing friends. It hurts big time. Slowly, I'm finding a remedy!

Many women I've talked with have gone through the same thing. We all agree on one piece of advice: make new friends. Over time, you'll come to see that your circle has new depth with people who understand you now. And you'll be able to bless the relationships you've lost, and truly let them go.

Our relationship with ourselves goes through so many changes during separation and divorce that it stands to reason our relationships with those around us will naturally change as well. And while that's nicely said on paper, in real life it can be a huge undertaking with emotional turmoil attached. Adding insult to injury, these relationship changes can also come at a point in the divorce when there's no going back to the marriage and life feels really, really, really hard. You just may want to pull your hair out.

But I'm here to tell you, you can do this! It's another act of surrendering to what's in front of you. Here we go…

Your Changing Relationship with Yourself

One of the interesting pieces about life is that, divorce or no divorce, things *keep* changing. So while we may have ideas and expectations about *how we will feel* or *how our life will look* post divorce, chances are it won't be that way. As an example, I moved into a nice apartment while separating. I was totally okay there, until the rent kept going up. Finally, to be in integrity with myself, I decided to move, again. And so I did, even though it took a lot of soul searching and pride swallowing to admit that I needed to do that. The point is, we get to keep adjusting *how* our reality meets our expectations. And during a divorce, we get to do that *a lot.*

The process of self-discovery during and after divorce requires huge amounts of patience and a time commitment. Yet, when we undertake it willingly, it produces gold for us. We truly get to uncover what we need to make our lives not only livable, but enriched and full of passion. Remember, that what your friend or neighbor needs is not necessarily what you need. You are a unique person with unique desires. And, as women we're typically the glue in our family. How easy it is to get lost in everyone else's needs. It's so important to take time out every day to communicate with yourself—and who you're becoming now. Paying attention to those needs will carry you farther down the road of having a fulfilling life.

For many of us, it's incredibly, deeply painful to go through a divorce— one of the most painful experiences in a lifetime. All of our self-identity gets stripped to the bare bones, and there are many times we're faced with gripping anxiety. Many women, myself included, have a moment when they accept the pain of the grief and chaos. For some women, it's not one moment, but a series of gut-wrenching moments of accepting that all is not as we would wish. Yet when we're willing to sit with our pain and cry the tears that need to come, healing does happen.

One of the biggest changes we make is becoming a single parent, and for many of us now co-parenting as well. Several clients have reported a positive shift in their parenting. Joe expressed, "As soon as we separated,

I felt more confident in my parenting. I no longer questioned myself as much and the kids responded well to my being direct." Single parenting is hugely stressful, as many of us know. Some of my clients have tales of crawling into bed with a dirty house, dirty dishes in the sink, and bills left to be paid. It truly seems at times there's not enough time in a week to accomplish what we want, all while parenting our children and needing to give huge amounts of ourselves to that effort. Even more than the stress is the worry that the children will live into the stigma of "children of divorce", meaning they'll be traumatized or at a disadvantage for the rest of their lives.

For some of my clients this worry leads right into anxiety. "Before I divorced I just didn't have so much to worry about. Now I worry constantly and my heart races at times from all the stress", said Sharon. This is a time to de-stress with a warm bath and your favorite relaxation audio. As single parents, our children need us to parent ourselves well. If we weren't grown up before divorce, we get to fully grow up now.

When it comes to co-parenting, my experience is that when issues flare up for myself and my ex, it's a smaller version of what I felt during the divorce—overwhelm, anger, my justifying my actions, etc. The flurry doesn't last as long as it used to, thank goodness, but it's still a huge interruption in my life. There's still emotional "recovery" to go through. Typically there's something to buy that wasn't covered in the settlement or some change to the custody arrangement. When these changes come up, we get to figure it out with our ex, which means more conversations. When you add that to just having disentangled a marriage, it can feel like walking into the lion's den. The best we can hope for is to stay calm ourselves, so we'll have a clear head to communicate effectively.

Despite these trials of single parenting, most clients report opening up to more in their life after divorce—whether it's around spirituality, healthier relationships, finding work that's fulfilling, or all of the above. We humans are so resilient! Now each of these clients had their moments of doubt and anger, to be sure. And yet they're each still walking their walk. It takes a great deal of courage to be willing to change our view of ourselves. Yet that's exactly the work that's here to do. Most of all, it takes a willing heart and stepping out of our comfort zone again and again.

Joan shared her story: "I walked out with $700, two girls, and no job. I moved in with my sister. I got a job that was easy to get, a sales job selling cookware. Then they hired me to do trainings and I got a guaranteed check. Next I worked part time as a teacher's assistant, but I had to leave in the fall so my daughter could start school. And I had to go on welfare. I had been a teacher's assistant and then I was on welfare for two months; then I went back to school for nine months and learned computers. Ever since, I've been able to support myself. I'm doing great. I don't have a lot of money but you don't need a lot to be great."

I've also met many women who've gone on to start and run successful businesses. They talk about happier relationships now that include a lot of communication. A client, Roger, noted that he was enjoying a relationship where the communication is important to both of them and at a mature level. For the first time in his life, he's experiencing the benefits of communicating well with a partner. He's still astounded by this, and he's not alone. It's a common theme I hear from those who are dating after divorce. They say they don't take their dating relationships for granted, and they really enjoy a high degree of communication.

For many women I've spoken with going through a divorce, there's a sense that they see a bigger picture in front of them, calling them forth. Some have described it as needing a bigger fishbowl to play in, creating a life that was larger than the one they're leaving behind.

I've met powerful women who've decided to take on having more children as a single mother because that's their dream. Imagine finding a new way to make your dreams come true. These women are not stopping just because they don't have a partner. And I find that truly courageous. We step out of our comfort zone to find new work, to make new friends, to deal with all the choices needing to be made every day. We no longer live in the illusion that having someone by our side means "all is well".

Your Changing Relationship with Your Children

The tears are flowing again. How do I cope with not seeing my child when she's with her Dad? It's super hard. Although I know our custody arrangement is the best for us, sometimes I feel like I'm walking around in a shell; my armor is thick over my heart with grief. Any "arrangement" sucks. And as my shell softens, the tears fall, slowly at first, but like a river flowing to the ocean, they pick up speed until they're tumbling forth and my body lets loose. My body and heart know that the way through is to cry these tears. But my mind and ego just want to be strong. Something tells me there's strength in the surrendering to the grief and I've seen the truth of that. I'm able to make huge strides in my life when I accept the truth and the pain. But it doesn't make it easier to swallow my pride and say I'm divorced.

What's so hard for me is not having the intact family that I dreamt of in my childhood and had for several years. I grew up loving those summer moments of peace and calm in the backyard at dusk. I want that again—with family around me and a sense of belonging and feeling abundant love. These are the moments when I felt deeply that "all is well". Children, however, have a different way of knowing "all is well". They test and they fight, wanting boundaries. And when there isn't a united front between co-parents, they test and fight all the more.

Certainly the process of telling your children you're divorcing and then following through is one of the most gut-wrenching conversations you'll ever have. And children in different age ranges need to be told differently and will have different questions. I know it sounds ironic, but if you keep in the forefront of your mind one question, you'll survive. Keep asking yourself, "How can I support my child through this?" Some days the answer will be to talk openly and honestly. Other days the answer will be to buy your child a new dresser and more clothes for the other house. Another day the answer may be to seek support through their school counselor. Keep asking the question.

I can't stress enough the importance of good communication with your children. When your communication with them is strong and honest, they'll feel more secure that you're there for them. This takes a lot of effort on your part to strengthen communication skills and know yourself well enough so you can talk clearly in the heat of the moment. I often tell my daughter, "I don't know; I have to think about it more. I've never been a parent before in this situation." That's an honest way of clearly communicating that I need more time or information to make a decision.

Children of divorced parents get to practice patience a lot. The trick is to know how to handle the frustration without feeling guilty. For myself, I do better when I remember it's her frustration, not mine. Then I can think about the issue with more clarity.

With my daughter, I focus on giving her choices that she has control over. That's the bright side for her. We've developed a ritual to smooth the rough edges of the days she changes houses. When she was younger, we'd drop by the Dollar Store and she was allowed to peruse and purchase a small item. On a transition day after school, we now get a yogurt or grab a juice, always her choice. She looks forward to these outings. She has the power of choice built in and we also get a chance to connect.

I can see that her emotions build up and she's shifting psychologically to make the transition from Dad's house to Mom's house. Her parents are, after all, very different people. I watch her shift and sort to recover some ground where she can be present and loving with me, while still honoring her love for her dad. I've found it helps when I acknowledge what's up for her without an emotional charge. I might say, "Sounds like you had a great weekend with your Dad". A simple acknowledgment lets her know I'm okay with her loving her dad. Above all, our children need us to remind them that they don't have to choose one parent over the other. That's a big job for us.

If your child is having a lot of trouble adjusting to your divorce, invite help through seeking counseling for him/her. Your child may need to express how difficult it is to be doing homework with two people who have different styles. If he/she is over the age of seven and able to articulate issues, help him/her narrow in on exactly what's not working so a solution can be found. It's no surprise that many divorced parents have different parenting styles. Learning to find solutions for our children, although it takes time and sometimes help from a counselor, is worth the effort.

In keeping our children stable through our divorce, the first thing to keep in mind is that it's important to be in communication with your ex when it comes to your child's development. There are a myriad of things to talk about such as play dates, school projects, new friends, how your child is using their time, and how they're making decisions. Let's look at two areas, namely their friendships and their school experience.

Your Child's Friendships

When our children are very young, before they have a cell phone and can plan their own play dates, it's our job to help them socialize and discover new friendships. I'll be honest—this has been a tricky area for me. I tried to help my daughter find other friends whose parents were going through divorce too. She didn't really connect with any of them, so I stopped that approach, also in part due to the time crunch in life and the exhaustion of going through a divorce. In the end, she was getting plenty of love from the friends she already had. Try to avoid having your children only seeing certain friends at one house or the other. Over time, it's best if their friends can see your children's entire life. This may take some time as the sting of all the change wears off for everyone.

It's important to keep asking your children what they need. It helps to create a time when they know they can talk openly. We have so many opportunities to be out and about doing things. Yet as a family going through intense changes, I've found creating downtime at home invites a wonderful opportunity to discuss what's working or not for my child. Create these spaces in your life so your children can connect with you.

Your Child's School Experience

Your children's school life is a huge part of their foundation in life. Knowing that children crave stability and consistency, hopefully your child will be able to stay in their same school with the same set of friends while their family life is changing. My experience has been that it's worth the effort to do whatever it takes to make that happen.

Your child's teacher's number one goal is to support your child. That makes it our job to help the teacher accomplish that. What's helpful is direct communication, not expecting the teacher to be your friend, and recognizing that the teacher doesn't want to get caught in the middle of your divorce. Make sure all communications involve the teacher, you, and your ex. Mail that comes home through your child's backpack is challenging. We have to stay on top of asking our children what papers came home today. This is when it's good to have another mom friend in the class who you can ask about upcoming events to stay in the loop.

Many children will feel alienated from their peers just because their family is going through a divorce. They may begin lashing out at others or their teachers as a response. Other children will over achieve as a way of coping and staying under the radar. There's still stigma in being from a newly divorced family, especially for children. My suggestion is to keep looking for support from people who are open to communicating about the issues rather than just watching from a distance. You may find a family going through a similar change and arrange pizza night together where everyone is able to talk and be heard.

Sometimes it may feel like all eyes are on *you* when you're on the school grounds. And believe me, they are at times. It's hard to feel like everyone knows your business, but in the interest of our children, we forge ahead. The fruit of our behind-the-scenes work to clear the emotional baggage with our ex will show up at Back to School Night. My ex and I just got back to the point where we can sit together at the school concert. Big step forward. And our daughter was so happy to come out and see that!

What will my child remember of her childhood? What will she hold on to as important? Although these questions are important, it's more powerful to stay in the now. I focus on what I *can* create with her now. Staying in the moment when I'm with her gives her the best of me. I'm looking forward to a 4th of July BBQ and fireworks with my daughter and friends—new friends, friends who understand the pain of separation and divorce. We take great comfort in one another.

Your Changing Relationship with Your Ex

Disentangling from your ex is kind of like having a baby. People can tell you all about it, but until you go through it, you just don't know the pain involved or exactly how it will go. For some, the dissolution goes smoothly, especially if both partners are ready to separate. For others, the divorce may drag on for years. Read on for hints so your divorce doesn't fall into the latter category.

For many couples, the largest piece of dissolving the marriage that creates the most disharmony is agreeing on the settlement. So I'd like you to think of your divorce as having two stages: getting to the divorce and life after signing the papers.

Getting to the Divorce

The most important piece to remember is that this phase won't last forever. For many divorcing couples, there will be power struggles. The anger prevalent during a divorce can wreak havoc on a settlement. Typically the power struggles are around finances and children. Now who among us doesn't want to have more time with our children and who doesn't want more money? So at some point you have to ask yourself: what am I willing to let go of? Because staying in this stage longer prevents you from moving on after your divorce. Hopefully, after your divorce there will be fewer power plays and less animosity.

In the period where you're still divorcing, you'll want sound advice from your lawyer about what your options are in terms of your financial settlement. All the work you put into finding the right lawyer will pay off. Even though it's a difficult time, trusting your lawyer is so important. And there's also plenty of legwork to be done, appraisals to be had, accountants to be consulted. I encourage you to be highly vigilant in each area and know that it takes time. But procrastinating won't get it done either.

Life after Signing the Papers

It's common to feel euphoric after the divorce is over and the papers are signed. It's also common to feel hugely sad and depressed. After all, you've just lost an important relationship in your life. At least you're through the horrible, gut-wrenching stage of getting to it and through it. Now you have a chance to separate emotionally and create your own life that has meaning and resonance for you.

What To Do When Your Ex Despises You

Whew, this is one tough arena. I tackle it here because it's more common than you know. I've seen divorcing couples spewing verbal threats back and forth, even in front of the children. Don't let that be part of your story.

Learn to separate what's triggering you from your reactions. This can be a highly emotional time, yet all our responses don't need to come from that highly emotional place. This is the place to take an honest look at your own emotional reactions. Remember, the emotions involved will impact your future as well as your children's.

Doing the work of separating the triggers and reactions is trickier than just talking or reading about it. You may not notice you've been triggered until the day after an episode occurs and you're still playing the conversation in your head, and biting your lip, and fuming. Then, you recognize that hurling back an insult wasn't in your best interest. The challenge is to realize in the moment that you're feeling triggered—your heart rate rises, your palms are sweaty, and you may feel the urge to run, or worse, hit.

Dealing with your anger takes a lot of compassion. The Dalai Lama tells us to deal with anger through compassion and nonviolence. But how do you keep your tongue in check when the anger rises in your body like a huge wave that's dying to be ridden? The irony of course, is that one of the surest ways to deal with anger is by being compassionate with yourself. But that feels like bullshit head talk, doesn't it?

How then, can you truly, in the face of hurt and divorce, cultivate compassion?

My client Emily recently described a scenario that put her over the edge. She had put the phone down for the third time that morning. Again, she had been talking with her pending ex, hassling about the kids. Why couldn't he be reasonable about her needs to see the kids? And now her family was coming to town and he was being a pain about switching weekends. It felt like he was trying to make her pay all over again. She felt bitter, more bitter than she'd ever felt in her whole life. All she'd wanted was a loving relationship. Theirs had soooooo not been loving. It had been a huge act of trust to divorce. But she knew she deserved more from a relationship. She was beginning to lose hope that anyone could truly love another person in partnership.

What do you do when the anger arises? The moment the anger strikes is possibly not the best time to be wondering how to cultivate compassion. In the moment, as we pay attention to our body signals, we get clues about what's going on. For many, body temperature rises and the fight or flight mechanism takes over. Jill Bolte Taylor, the now famous neuroscientist who had a stroke and experienced nirvana, says the initial flash of anger only lasts 90 seconds. From there, we have a choice about how to handle it. How we handle that 90 seconds says a lot about who we are. How far have we come from caveman days?

What to Do: Count to 5

Forget 10. This is a crazy, busy society. Count to five and do your best to calm down. Notice your heightened sense of awareness, and take deep breaths to calm down. Flash upon something pleasurable in your mind. Remember, reacting negatively can take more time and energy than you probably want to give to this situation.

What to Do: Speak Your Mantra

You need a mantra, baby. Pull the mantra out and repeat it over and over in your mind when confronted by a difficult situation. Paying attention to where you focus can be THE shift between a 90-second anger burst and a 90-minute downward spiral. I'm betting your time is precious.

Some mantra suggestions:

> ➢ I'm calm here and now.
> ➢ I create my reality.
> ➢ I'll get through this; I just need to breathe.
> ➢ This is temporary.
> ➢ Create your own here: _____.

What to Do: Pause, Please…

Ask for the pause. You don't have to mention that you're angry, but asking to take a break gives you the space to talk about the issue from a place of control. "I can't talk about this now, but I'll call you back later."

Find Appropriate Outlets

Choose activities that will help you keep your stress level down. Strenuous physical activity is one sure way to get your blood flowing in a positive manner. It creates an outlet for letting the small stuff go. Have you ever noticed sometimes when exercising you replay the small worries and aches of life and they seem so insignificant?

A client of mine, Nadine, while recounting a story about her pending ex, spoke of how she wanted to thrash him and wring his neck. She laughed and we came up with the idea of having a "John" doll that she could take out and slaughter just for those moments when she was overwhelmed by anger about a situation. Now surely, this isn't something you let the kids see. And perhaps punching a pillow would work as well!

And above all, remember that this too will pass. Each moment turns into the next. Choose your responses, in the moment.

Another question to ask yourself when you feel your ex despises you is, "How can I separate further from this person?" Have you actually finished the divorce? If not, what needs to happen so you can? Are you still borrowing things back and forth, or are you standing completely on your own? For a couple of summers, my ex and I traded some camping gear back and forth until I realized I was out of integrity with myself. So I found a friend I could trade camping gear with and noticed the upcoming trips were much calmer in the days leading up to them.

Above all, the biggest question to ask yourself is, on a scale of 1 to 10, how much *do I* despise my ex? If the number is higher than 6, there's probably some work to be done around detaching, letting go, and forgiving. More on that later.

Keeping the Hope Alive

Relationships truly make the world go round. Give yourself plenty of spaciousness to dive into the following. With a cup of tea and your journal handy, answer these questions from your heart. For each category, create one action item for yourself.

Bronze

Journal about your changing relationship with yourself. (See questions below.) Choose one action item to complete.

Silver

Journal about your changing relationship with yourself and your changing relationship with your children. (See questions below.) Choose one action item for each area and complete them.

Gold

Journal about your changing relationship with yourself, your children, and your ex. (See questions below.) Choose one action item for each area and complete them.

Relationship with Yourself

How are you opening to receive in your life now? How are you meeting your need for touch, love, and laughter? What artistic, spiritual, or exercise practices sustain and feed you? How do you know when you need support? How do you know when you're okay?

Three suggestions for action:

1. Give yourself an art afternoon where you can draw, paint, or make a necklace. Keep it simple!
2. Grab a friend and do yoga in your living room.
3. Schedule a massage.

Relationship with Children

Put yourself in your children's shoes. What are they feeling? What's going well for them? What do you need to let go of so your children are less stressed? Who do they feel they can talk with? What would be most helpful to them? What guilt can you let go of?

Three suggestions for action:

1. Schedule a chat with your children's teacher.
2. Set aside 30 minutes to take your children to the park.
3. Create a transition ritual with your children where they get to voice what they need as they move from house to house.

Relationship with Ex

What boundaries need to be redrawn? What is the next step for you in separating from your partner? What is your ex right about that you haven't owned up to?

Three suggestions for action:

1. Write a forgiveness letter to your ex. If you're not ready to send it, release the energy by burning it.
2. Ask your ex to coffee *without* having an agenda.
3. Commit to praying for your ex for three months.

Affirmations

I love and accept myself as I am.
I honor all my relationships.

CHAPTER 6

Sacred Community Circles
Redefining Family

∾

While the spirit of neighborliness was important on the
frontier because neighbors were so few, it is even more
important now because our neighbors are so many.
~Lady Bird Johnson

Your Changing Relationship with Extended Family

The loss of my extended family was difficult for me. My ex forbade his family from having contact with me. In short, I was outlawed from the in-laws. I quickly lost my mother-in-law, whom I adored and who was a lot like me (go figure)! There were plenty of times I called my in-laws when my child was visiting them only to be treated with disrespect. The irony is that all my adult in-laws had been through a divorce too. No matter what we think may happen to these relationships, we never truly know how it will pan out.

So be prepared. You may possibly lose your relationship with your entire extended family. Your relationship with your own family may change too as they begin to look at you as a woman going through divorce. If they've been through a divorce too, this can bring up their own fears about their past divorce and about whether or not their life is better post divorce.

Be clear about *your* issues being separate from others' stories. I encourage you to keep asking specifically for what you need. Often our parents are fearful *for* us when what we need is acceptance for where we're at right now. I could feel my mother's anxiety about my divorce through the telephone line, and often she didn't settle down until she came to see me once or twice a year. Hopefully, your family can help you out by being willing to talk about what's going on—whether in person, or phone, or even email.

When my mother came to town while I was going through my divorce, she still wanted to see my ex. But that made me uncomfortable. *After* my divorce, I no longer felt uncomfortable about her seeing him. Be aware that their relationship is changing too, and it will go through different stages.

Plan ahead for the holidays with your own family as much as possible. When you have a big holiday without your kids, you may not want to show up to your family function. Or that may be just what you need. Be gentle with yourself and recognize what feels supportive and what doesn't, acknowledging even that can change on a dime. Do your best to maintain open relationships with everyone so you get your needs met.

Notes for Girlfriends

So your friend is going through a divorce, eh? She's going to need a lot of support to get through and rebuild her life. Let's face it, it's scary to start over. So many things may have changed for your friend. She may be living in a new place, driving a different car, looking for work, and worrying about shoring up her children's emotional health, all at the same time. Following are some tips to help you see your friend through this time.

This is helpful for your friend:

- ✓ Invite her to dinner.
- ✓ Provide resources.
- ✓ Suggest she see a professional when you're tired of listening to her "story".
- ✓ Invite her to group functions, even if she has to turn you down.
- ✓ Remember her at holidays.
- ✓ Keep inviting her children to play dates and functions.
- ✓ Extend an invitation to anyone she's dating too.
- ✓ Be forgiving of her lack of being the "best friend".
- ✓ Ask her what you can do to help.

This is not helpful for your friend:

- ❑ Don't speak poorly of her ex, even if/when she does.
- ❑ Don't expect her always to call back right away.
- ❑ Don't assume anything, including that she's "OK now".

Lana Foladare, M.A., C.P.C.C.

Your Changing Relationship with Your Community

People react in all kinds of ways to those of us going through divorce. What's important to remember is that everyone has their story. My client Susan summed it up nicely saying, "The hardest thing for me to deal with is watching how the children of my former friends take on the apparent 'story' of their families in regard to divorce. There are children among my son's friends who act really timid and afraid of me now. I can only imagine how the conversation has gone at their house in regard to divorce. So far, the best antidote has been to kindly remind myself that they're loving children taking on the stories of their parents. So I do my best to respond in kind and keep focused where I need to be in that moment, which is on the kids' relationships. It feels sad to know that I've lost friends. Losing a marriage is tough, and then losing the friends I thought I had, feels staggering. To pile it on, when I see people and they act excited about the positive changes I've made, I know my old friends are talking about me. But they're no longer inviting *me* to *that* conversation! I just have to keep going, making new friends or I'll starve my heart of affection."

I've noticed that adults I know who've been through their own divorce or their parents' divorce often have difficulty keeping a long term relationship with me now too. People get triggered, and it's my job to remember that's their stuff. I can ask them about it and engage them in conversation. But I'm finding their reaction to my situation is often not about me, it's about their unresolved issues.

On the positive side, I've noticed how the friends coming into my life now aren't afraid to talk about what's difficult for them in their lives. Thank goodness! They're also going through this transition of being single again. "I no longer sit in a restaurant and see all the people as couples," said Nadine. "Now I understand their relationships are more complex too, and half of them either have been divorced or may be in the future." Imperfections abound during a divorce. Somehow it's more joyful to meet people and start from current time.

For me, going through divorce has meant a reprioritizing of so many things. My brain has shifted, and things I thought I wouldn't be able to live with, I now find I can. What helps the most is having friends with open minds and hearts who understand pain and loss.

Unfortunately you may lose friendships during your divorce. We've all heard the saying about friends only being in our lives for a season. I've found that to be true, especially during times of transition. Your ex may even have picked up what you thought of as "your friends". Even though it hurts, you have to move on.

Keeping the Hope Alive

Bronze

Journal about your changing relationship with your extended family. (See questions below.) Choose one action item to complete.

Silver

Journal about your changing relationship with your extended family and your changing relationship with your community. (See questions below.) Choose one action item for each area and complete them.

Gold

Journal about your changing relationship with your extended family and your community. (See questions below.) Choose two action items for each area and complete them.

Relationship with Extended Family

What have you and your ex decided about contact with in-laws after divorce? Is it what you want? Who can you discuss this with to get your needs met? Do you need to say goodbye to extended family you may never see again?

Three suggestions for action:

1. Reach out to a woman in your family lineage and confess what's hardest for you right now.

2. Call one of your ex in-laws and have a truth-telling moment from your heart.
3. Tell your child a favorite story of something that happened with your ex's family.

Relationship with Community

Take stock of your current friendships. How can you make them stronger? Which ones need to be set free? Who do you most need to take to coffee or go on a walk with?

Three suggestions for action:

1. Write a blessing letter to the friendships you've lost.
2. Schedule coffee with that friend you most need.
3. Strike up a conversation with someone new.

Affirmations

I radiate love and happiness.

I am surrounded by love.

CHAPTER 7

Prophecy Revealed
5 Steps to Getting CLEAR

I'm not much of a partier anymore. I enjoy clarity much more.
~ Sheryl Crow

It takes courage to walk through divorce, whether you wanted the divorce or not. For most women I've spoken with, there comes a time when they begin to see new glimpses of what's possible for their life. For some, that comes before they got divorced. For others, this happens maybe two thirds of the way through the divorce, when things are still quite hard emotionally. It's almost a gift to be given a sign that something new is emerging. It helps us to face the bigger picture, even when it's not all rosy.

I devised a system of getting **CLEAR** to facilitate these times when we're not sure whether we're moving forward or moving backward. We'll work with this later in the chapter. For now, the **C-L-E-A-R** steps are:

1) **C**reate a Goal
2) **L**ist Action Steps
3) **E**nlist Encouragement
4) **Ac**cept What Is
5) **R**epeat Steps 1-4

As we begin to see glimpses of what's around the corner for us, it can feel like a time of back and forth. Before we really move on to the next stage, we go back and forth, looking at what was and what we envision is to come. Often, this is accompanied by children literally going back and forth

73

between houses as well. So for those of us with children, we're reminded frequently of what *was* if we're still seeing our ex. This is the time when everyone is adjusting to something new. It's not so brand new anymore that it's even interesting. And sometimes it feels exhausting, because there isn't the new life or dream fully in place—yet!

Depression is anger turned inward, as opposed to being expressed. Everyone has anger. It's really not a terrible thing. It's how we express our anger that can have consequences. So cliché, I know, but rather hit a pillow or the couch than a person or a child. Better to admit the anger and find an outlet than have it impact your other relationships. "Sometimes I just feel so Rrrrrrrrr, like I'm going to explode," said my client Carl as he was working through feelings around being forced into a custody schedule he didn't like.

Taking that first step of identifying where you're at with your anger is paramount. It's like a fence that's there—it's not going to go away. Your job is to see which side you're on for any given day. Is today about being angry or expressing it? Just like when you climb a fence and you're at the top, you get to choose which side to come down on. Choosing the side where you express yourself keeps you nimble so you can keep choosing personal expression, rather than depression.

For one client, Kara, the holidays were now better, two years after the separation had begun. "This past weekend, my son was with his dad and his family. Since we've all been through the holiday split before, it doesn't feel so devastating. We know what to expect. Jack was really looking forward to being with his cousins. Mostly, I try to not make him feel torn between loving me and feeling sorry for me because I'm missing him and my past extended family too.

"Now that he's old enough to text from his own phone, our communication is more frequent when he's away. And I don't have to go through his dad anymore to talk to him. I keep things light on the phone and let Jack know what I'm up to. It's good for him to know I have a life without him, with friends, and staying busy, etc."

Realize that it's important to plan things while the kids are away, as well as to have some downtime. Yes, it's another juggling act, meeting new friends, and wanting to be in a happy lighthearted space to actually enjoy them. This is an area where a lot of us get to grow our patience quota for ourselves!

For another client, Sasha, it had been four years since she separated and she was still grieving. "I recently moved, again, for the second time in three years. Some people are giving me grief about it. Like didn't you just move? Yes, one year ago, that's correct."

What Sasha found most important was to keep focusing on the positive. "So much of picking myself up after my divorce has to do with recovering my self-esteem. It's strange that now I can pick out the thoughts I have that are based on low self-esteem. Post-divorce life can be scary and rewarding all in the same moment. My spiritual practices that remind me to stay present to each moment, right here, right now, have been a big part of getting me through sanely."

What an eye opener it is to detangle our lives from someone we shared so much with. At every first pass of a holiday or birthday, our brain wants to re-enact old stories. Take some time when you reach a new milestone to honor the loss of your spouse. Even though I'd been divorced for a year, some part of me wanted to show my ex my new office! After all, he'd been there for other new offices of mine. I acknowledged this, and then I invited new friends and associates to gather 'round me to celebrate my space.

For Julia, it had been 18 months since she'd been thrown into her divorce. She had begun to feel that something new awaited her. Although she wasn't sure whether it was work related or relationship related, it brightened her mood and called her forth.

An important piece of the process of dissolving her marriage lay in rediscovering her values. "John and I had become glued at the hip on weekends. I could no longer tell if we were doing things because he wanted to or I wanted to. We'd developed our routines, and that's just how things were. Boy, was I in for a shock having a weekend to myself. And now, I have every other weekend to myself. It's especially difficult for me when he has the children and I'm alone. I barely know what to do with myself. And I'm scared of trying new things. Trying one new thing a month is a huge deal for me. I move from paralysis to tears to baby steps. And then I'm so tired and grumpy from dealing with all of that. Does this ever get easier? This living alone and finding a new life?"

Yes, is the answer. And how soon it gets easier depends in part on how much support we get and the new things we try. So Julia and I embarked upon a journey of understanding who she is now and what's valuable to her now. She was surprised at how much of what she'd been doing with John really held no interest for her any more. They used to laze around on Sundays, but for years she'd wanted to check out her local church. So she did with a plan in place to meet one new person. And that was easy. Within three months, she had checked out two other churches as well and found a fit. She was on her way to becoming a member at her new spiritual home.

One of the biggest blocks Julia overcame was sitting around thinking about the way things had been. Instead of starting her weekends off on the wrong foot, she set a conscious intention to create something new for herself. Even when she was down with a cold, she created the same intention and saw that she wasn't as hard on herself or using negative self-talk even when she didn't feel well.

Julia enjoyed discovering what was truly important to her now. She continued to find that activities she *thought* she enjoyed, she no longer did. And more importantly she found the courage to try new things to do—that she genuinely enjoyed.

So how do we move from the paralysis and fear of what divorce might bring to a place of acceptance and willingness to create something new? Again, getting **CLEAR** means to:

1) **C**reate a Goal
2) **L**ist Action Steps
3) **E**nlist Encouragement
4) **Ac**cept What Is
5) **R**epeat Steps 1-4

For someone in the process of divorce, this may look like:

1) Hire financial planner
2) Do these action steps:
a) Poll three friends for recommendations
b) Make phone calls by Tuesday
c) Set up appointment for Friday
3) Tell friends what I'm up to
4) Person I want to see can't see me until Monday
5) Set new goal based on current schedules

Your goals come out of your values. Values are what make life unique to you. People are "the way they are" because of the values they live by. Consider the following two different **Top 10 Values** lists of Candice and Amy. Notice how they would make each woman's life unique and different from the other.

Candice

➔ Abundance
➔ Balance
➔ Candor
➔ Fitness
➔ Fun
➔ Giving
➔ Passion
➔ Reliability
➔ Self-control
➔ Trust

Amy

- ➲ Belonging
- ➲ Diversity
- ➲ Exploration
- ➲ Family
- ➲ Growth
- ➲ Integrity
- ➲ Learning
- ➲ Open-mindedness
- ➲ Perseverance
- ➲ Resourcefulness

Take a minute now to determine your top three values. Look over the list below. Write in any values important to you that aren't listed. For other ideas, look at the lists above or look at the list of 175 values in The Resources section in the back of this back.

Authenticity
Friendship
Family
Fame
Happiness
Integrity
Joy
Love
Peace
Power
Recognition
Status
Success
Truth
Wealth
Wisdom

_____

_____

List your top eight values here:

1.

2.

3.

4.

5.

6.

7.

8.

Of those eight, now list your top five:

1.

2.

3.

4.

5.

Of those five, now list your top three:

1.

2.

3.

Now, on a scale of 1 (lowest) to 10 (highest), rate how well you're living these three values.

Setting goals that honor the values of reliability and trust may look very different from goals that honor learning and family. Consider what values you've been honoring lately and what values you'd like to honor more.

The alchemy we create has a lot to do with what values we hold dear and the goals we create from those. For some women going through divorce, this transformational change is around their spiritual life. "Before the divorce I felt I was always a part of something, as a daughter, or a wife," said Gina. "And then I went through a period where I learned that I was going to be okay on my own, even after that dream I was clutching was taken from me. Now I'm finding out who I am."

It's amazing that how we define ourselves—our self-constructs—are hardwired into our bodies and routines. For Gina, shopping at the grocery store was a place she confronted her newfound singleness weekly. "I'd go into the store, and all of a sudden I was very aware that I was shopping for one person. And I wondered if other people knew that too. I hadn't shopped for one person ever before in my life. I was overcome with sadness right there in the produce department. I kept thinking, who am I now? And who does everyone see? I had been so happy before."

Women who need to go back to work post-divorce have to give up the myth that the Prince is going to rescue them. This honors the value of financial responsibility. "My husband used to take care of all the bills, and I never had to worry or budget," said Lisa. "Now I'm struggling to make ends meet, and see I need to be making more money. I understand that not only do I need to work, but I *want* to work. There has to be something more fulfilling out there for me." Many who get divorced in their 40s may finally decide to dig in to work they love—their heart's calling.

Sandra followed the steps to getting **CLEAR** and landed a job that honored her value of financial responsibility. Knowing her end goal was to be employed, she created smaller goals to get there.

Her steps looked like this:

Create a Goal	1) Rewrite resume by Friday.
List Action Steps	2) Look at other resumes; begin writing by Monday.
Enlist Encouragement	3) Get input from friends.
Accept What Is	4) Buy paper and ink for printer.
Repeat Steps 1-4	5) Resume done! Back to one.

Create a Goal	1) Apply for five positions.
List Action Steps	2) Get online; update LinkedIn profile; make calls to reconnect with associates.
Enlist Encouragement	3) Watch movie "Rudy"; tell three others what I'm up to.
Accept What Is	4) This is taking longer than I'd hoped. Build in daily exercise routine to keep spirits up.
Repeat Steps 1-4	5) Re-commit to build enthusiasm.

Sandra's smaller goals were things like getting help with her resume or applying for five positions. The momentum started growing, and along the way, she got encouragement from her coach and her family. She was rejected more than once and accepted that for what it was (step 4). She kept moving forward in her job search and landed a job that both met her needs and excited her. Along the way, she experienced substantial personal growth. She became more patient, action-oriented, and self-loving.

Divorce in our mid-40s can be a touchstone to why we're on the planet. One client, Amelia, turned to astrology and meditation to find answers for herself. "I was racked with these questions of what now, and what am I here for? I couldn't sleep at night any more thinking about all the people on the planet in need. My current life seemed a bit mundane and disconnected to the greater good. So I decided to do something about it. That's the only way I could sleep well again. Getting into action helped me turn the corner on my life. I now have meaningful work and I look forward to each day."

Keeping the Hope Alive

Bronze

Turn to the list of values in the Resources section and identify your top 10 values now. On a scale of 1 (lowest) to 10 (highest), rate how well you're living your values. Identify one action you'll take to bring those numbers up.

Silver

Do the values exercise as listed in bronze and name three new activities you've been wanting to do that will increase your rating. Make a plan to do these activities *within the next month*.

Gold

Complete the exercises for silver. In your journal, answer these questions:

> 1) What do I need to move forward?
> 2) How do I know when I'm stuck?
> 3) How has my patience grown?
> 4) What keeps me from asking for help?
> 5) Whom do I truly trust?

Affirmations

I'm worthy, right here, right now.

I believe in me!

CHAPTER 8

Speaking in Tongues
Legal Jargon

❦

Turn your wounds into wisdom.
~ Oprah Winfrey

The following information about different ways to divorce has elicited lengthy discussions from the women in my workshops who are at the early end of divorcing. I include this information here as a cursory glimpse of getting started and what you need to know. There are many ways to divorce and it pays to educate yourself around the logistics of this. To simplify this conversation, I'm going to show you four ways to divorce and I'll show you how they each rate on the expense scale. Also, we'll briefly look at different custody situations for your children.

Four Types of Divorce

1. DIY Method, or Do It Yourself. The *pros* of this are that it's the most affordable option. DIY is a valid option for those couples who have no children, no properties, and no assets. It's the easiest way to split nothing. The *con* of DIY is that if you make a mistake, it can be very costly. One of my clients, before she found me, was using the DIY method by representing herself in court even though her husband had a lawyer. She believes it cost her time with her daughter on a regular basis, because she wasn't adequately prepared and the judge sided with her husband. Costly!

Others have made mistakes in the DIY process and had to hire legal help anyway to get it fixed. You'll be responsible for preparing and filing all of your own documents. But if done right, and you and your pending ex agree on how to split things, and if there's still enough trust between you to get the deal signed, it can be a valid option.

2. Mediation. Ah, it seems a few years ago everyone was moving toward mediation. On the positive end, mediation can save you money, because the two of you are hiring one person, a mediator, to help you work out a deal. And the deal can be quite flexible, as long as you agree. Maybe you want the house and he wants an account. In this scenario, you can negotiate with each other for what you want. Though you'll want separate attorneys to review your agreement prior to signing. But that's still less expensive than having two divorce lawyers work on your divorce.

On the negative side, remember that the mediator's goal is to act neutral and help the parties make a deal. And it's divorce, so it's not going to feel good or fair. After all, you're splitting the pie. If there was an imbalance of power before in the relationship (who knows the intricate details of the family's accounting and who doesn't?), that imbalance will still be present in these negotiations. That's a big con for many women who haven't paid attention to the family finances. They most likely aren't going to be able to speak up for themselves at the mediation table. Whatever communication patterns were happening or not during the marriage, this is the same communication that's brought to the mediation or divorce table. The mediator can't balance the power. Sad, but true.

3. Collaborative Law. This is the latest and greatest in the divorce arena. In this scenario, each person has a team composed of a lawyer and a coach with whom they attend meetings. So imagine six people sitting around a table hammering out the deal without huge blows. Not bad, huh? Your coach helps you keep your emotions in check, since dividing up a marriage can be hugely difficult, and thereby emotional. They can also advise you on issues affecting your children.

On the positive side for collaboration, these meetings keep your divorce out of court so *you're* making the decisions for your future, the custody of your children, etc. And you have your own lawyer, as opposed to mediation. On the negative side, it can be more costly than mediation in the short term, but perhaps well worth it if there are communication issues that might prevent you from showing up equally to the dividing table.

4. Litigation. Lastly, you have the traditional litigation with lawyers working a settlement or going to trial and you paying the bill (or your spouse if you can negotiate for that). We've all heard horror stories of friends' divorces that ended up here. On the up side, with a good lawyer on your side, your divorce will get done. But it may take a long time, as in two to three years. You're at the behest of the court system and their setting dates for your case. You'll go through court mediation to decide what you want for your children, but in the end, the judge will have the last word.

This type of divorce can be lengthy and costly. However, if your pending ex hires a power attorney, you'd better do the same. And be open to mixing and matching the above options. It's entirely possible that you, your ex, and your two lawyers can sit together and strike a deal. No matter whom you work with, make sure you can trust him/her. They're going to know A LOT about you by the time this is over.

The tough part is agreeing as a divorcing couple on which type of divorce will work for you. I'll say it again, because it's so important: **The tough part is agreeing as a divorcing couple on which type of divorce will work for you.**

Once you've got the process chosen, if you need to, you can find the right lawyer by looking for:

- Someone who listens to you, who you can be honest with.
- Someone who has a good track record in your particular issues: custody, property, etc.
- Someone you can build rapport with who can hold their own against your ex's lawyer.

Custody Situations

Custody arrangements take many different forms. What's most important is to find something that everyone buys into, to some degree. There are two types of custody to settle: legal custody and physical custody. Legal custody is about who has the right to make decisions for the children on medical care, education, and religious upbringing. Physical custody declares who the children will live with after the divorce.

It's important to work these arrangements out with your pending ex, either through your lawyers, a mediator, or divorce coaches. If you allow the custody piece of your divorce to go before a judge, you're allowing strangers to dictate what will happen with the future of your children. Most custody cases are now settled out of court, so you have lots of company.

Legal Custody

The two options for legal custody are Primary Custody and Joint Custody. Even if one of you has primary custody, certain decisions may be made by both of you. Primary custody can be awarded if one parent has been solely responsible for the upbringing of the child. In joint custody situations, you're agreeing to agree on major issues for your children. Where they go to school, what church they go to, and what type of medical care they receive are all issues to be discussed and agreed on when you have joint custody.

To decide what you think is best, take into consideration that having a lengthy court battle over legal custody will have lasting effects on how your children grow up establishing relationship ties. Take a divorce co-parenting class and talk with others, as well as your lawyer, to get ideas about how people in similar situations are handling the difficult decisions. Better to diffuse your anger at your ex rather than have it thrown into the custody battle.

Physical Custody

As kids get older, they want more say in their schedule so they can be with their friends. It's best to keep the lines of communication with your children open so they feel comfortable talking about their relationship needs. Remember, every physical custody arrangement will have changes and slip-ups. It's best if you can be flexible when work and travel schedules conflict with your court document. Hopefully, you and your ex will still have a degree of trust between you so your children aren't constantly caught in the middle.

When you enter into an arrangement, it's important to clarify for yourself the issue of time versus custody share. Most children will be in school during weekdays, so think about what quality time you'll have with them. Weekends are prime for that, weekdays not so much. So an arrangement where your child sees one parent most weekends and the other parent during the week is separating one of the parents from most of the fun times. Often I hear women wanting to keep control of the child's week and homework situation. That can lead to disappointment over the long run, as there's little time left for fun in their relationship.

Unfortunately, the anger of divorcing usually plays into deciding on the custody arrangement. This is where it pays to get support and separate the anger from the issues. Is your co-parent really a jerk? Is there any chance you can visualize your co-parent as responsible? This is where we need to take the highest road possible in the interest of the children.

If you can imagine it as a custody situation, somewhere someone is living it. Even if it sounds screwy to outsiders but you think it's going to work, give it a whirl. My ex and I ended up doing a 50/50 physical custody schedule of 2, 2, 5, 5. Unless you've heard the lingo before, it sounds like we've lost our minds. *But it works.* Let's take a further look.

Suggestions for a 50/50 Split of Physical Custody

1. One week at Dad's, one week at Mom's. You can schedule in a visit during the week that includes dinner and homework. This one works well for kids with lots of homework when the parents are on task in helping them accomplish that. The down side: it's a long time away from your child.

2. Two, two, five, five. Two days with Dad (Mon, Tues) and two days with Mom (Wed, Thurs). Then five days with Dad (F, S, S, M, T) and five days with Mom (W, Th, F, S, S). The upside here is you're alternating weekends, something I recommend highly so adults get their adult time. Also, the longest stretch without your child seeing you is five days. You can even schedule a visit in the middle of the five days, so the longest stretch becomes three days.

3. Some families might elect to have one parent cover all the weekends (F, S, S) with one evening as well, while the other parent covers the weekdays. Difference in the time share can be made up over the summer holidays.

Suggestions for a 70/30 Split of Physical Custody

1. The parent who has 70% takes weekdays and two weekends per month. The 30% parent takes every other weekend with an additional day, say Thursday, for consistency. So the children would be with the 30% parent on Th, F, S, S every other week.

2. Another option is to follow the example above, and instead of Thursdays, pick another day if you feel it's going to be too long without the children seeing one parent. Any extra time can be made up in the summer.

Most important is that you guard against having your child/ren feel very split. Of course, no one can chop a kid in half—but they'll feel like that at times. I caution families from creating schedules that contain too much back and forth, as in every day. This creates a great deal of upheaval for the children.

I also caution against scheduling too many holidays that you swap back and forth from year to year (for example, Thanksgiving with Mom odd years, with Dad even years). Let's face it, November through March, there's typically at least one major holiday per month. Instead of creating havoc with the swapping calendar, I suggest limiting the swapped holidays to the big three or four (Thanksgiving, Christmas, Easter). This is less grueling on the kids. Also, keep in mind whether or not you'll be seeing your ex during drop-offs and pick-ups. When the drop-off happens during the school day—for example, Dad drops off Wednesday morning and Mom has Wednesday evening—you don't have to see each other and therefore, there's less tension.

The most important thing you can do to claim your power at this stage is to make wise choices after getting educated.

Keeping the Hope Alive

Bronze

If you haven't yet chosen a lawyer, schedule initial conversations with two to get you started. If you have chosen a lawyer, complete whatever paperwork is outstanding at this time.

Silver

Complete the bronze exercises and journal about your bottom line deals on finances, custody, and property issues. What are you really not wanting to give up? What are you willing to give up? How do you anticipate being able to make peace with any gaps?

Gold

Complete the bronze and silver exercises. Journal about how you'll handle the stress of your divorce. What do you need to put into place regarding support, exercise, and career?

Affirmations

I speak my truth and walk my talk.

I make decisions with confidence.

CHAPTER 9

Finding Your Passionate Potion
Reclaiming Your Mojo

Life is not about waiting for the storms to pass.
It's about learning to dance in the rain!
~ Joyce Schneider

"After I first moved out, I literally had no idea what I truly liked and disliked anymore," said Maureen. "It was as if my constructs of who *I am,* were gone. I bought green grapes only to discover I really only like red grapes. If I was buying food for myself that I didn't like, *how many other things in my life were not true reflections of myself?*

"All of a sudden so many decisions felt paramount. The number of things I had to decide on was overwhelming. AND I had the power to make these decisions all by myself now, which is something I hadn't felt in my marriage.

"You see, during my marriage I had been living an illusion. I was kind of dead to life, just walking through it—you know, 2.5 kids and a dog kind of thing. I was unhappy, only I couldn't really tell you why. Since all my basic needs were being met, I wasn't very *un*comfortable, but I also wasn't fully ME."

Many women I speak with can relate to Maureen. As we move through our divorce, it's by taking small steps that we strengthen that muscle of determination to declare all of *who we are* to the world. Each stepping stone is a rite of passage itself.

Stepping Stones

✔ Spending nights alone again

✔ Taking yourself to dinner

✔ Finding new work to support yourself

✔ Making new friends

✔ Having coffee dates

✔ Really dating again

✔ Making love to someone new

"For me," said Joan, "the most difficult change has been to shift from being a stay-at-home mom to going into the world and earning my potential. I really enjoyed staying home when my kids were younger. This shift has also been the most powerful way I've recovered my sense of self, post-divorce. It's amazing the beliefs I was living with that were so untrue. I used to believe I couldn't make it in the working world or earn a decent living. Boy was I wrong. The hardest part was getting started with those first steps!

"I busted some of my big myths. I used to worry that the kids needed me home. I've discovered they're becoming more self-reliant as I encourage them to help me even more around the house now that I'm working outside the home again. By meeting other moms who work outside the home and hearing their stories, I'm encouraged. I've rearranged a lot of how I parent since I got divorced to fit my new lifestyle. We definitely stick to our routines of making lunches at night, and laying out clothes and backpacks too. Our new routines keep me sane and my children know what to expect. For me, it's no longer true that I need to be home so my children aren't traumatized from the divorce."

During this stage of divorce recovery, it's particularly important to walk the daily walk of affirming our values to create a new path and a new way of being. When we do that, we can rest assured that the life we're creating is uniquely ours. For many women, losing their soul to one marriage is enough. Yet time and again, I see women not making strong choices from what they truly need and ending up in a second marriage where they're resentful. This phase of divorce recovery may feel very long, lasting several years. And some get stuck here in bitterness, even if they wanted their divorce.

This is a time to literally reprogram our brains. We do this by honestly speaking up for our value-based needs, whether that's with family, an ex, at work, or home. It may feel funny at first making different choices that, at an earlier time, seemed so clear cut. Creating strong boundaries for ourselves lets us know we're safe. And when we feel safe, we can flourish, change, and grow.

> ### *I can be myself without*
> ### *the sky falling in.*

As we grow, there's a tendency to fall back into old patterns. A study in neural activity gives us concrete evidence of why we need support to establish new patterns. In the October 20, 2009 issue of *Nature*, a study led by Ann Graybiel of MIT's McGovern Institute, showed that important neural activity patterns in a specific area of the brain change when habits are formed, then change again when habits are broken. They quickly re-emerge when a trigger reawakens a former habit, one that originally took significant effort to learn.

Habits are helpful on a daily basis by eliminating the need to think about every little thing we do like tying our shoes or driving to work. Bad habits, however, can have a stranglehold on our mind and actions. Definitely difficult to break, they're unbelievably easy to restart.

"We knew that neurons can change their firing patterns when habits are learned, but it is startling to find that these patterns reverse when the habit is lost, only to recur again as soon as something kicks off the habit again," said Graybiel.

These patterns take place in the basal ganglia, a brain region essential to habits, addictions, and routine learning. "It is as though somehow, the brain retains a memory of the habit context, and this pattern can be triggered if the right habit cues come back," Graybiel said. "This situation is familiar to anyone who is trying to lose weight or to control a well-engrained habit." With a routine behavior, once we start, we run on autopilot, until we stop.

What all this means is when we make a change, we have to keep changing so the learning doesn't dissolve. To start creating new habits then, notice what habitual things you're doing that are creating negative self-talk for you. Maybe you've driven the same way to the grocery store for years. Try a new route.

Here are other suggestions to break the old patterns and create more of what you want. The key to each, however, is to notice what's going on with your self-talk. Don't create a new pattern that doesn't really work for you either!

- ❑ Change your morning routine of showering and getting ready. If you usually eat first, eat last. If you don't eat at all, eat!
- ❑ Sleep on the other side of the bed. Sleep with your head at your feet.
- ❑ If you have a favorite chair in the living room, move to another. Or move the furniture around.
- ❑ If you walk the dog, take a new direction, or jog.
- ❑ If you always call a friend, tell them you're experimenting and change what you talk about.
- ❑ If you have favorite TV shows, go one week without them, or watch something you've never seen before.

❑ If you've never eaten a certain vegetable, buy it and prepare it!
❑ If you "never" do something, do it!

To take care of the anxiety that can arise with change, I've used aromatherapy, exercise, massage, setting daily routines, the Emotional Freedom Technique (EFT), and anxiety reduction audios. At your natural foods store, you can purchase a car diffuser for less than $15 which plugs directly into your car's lighter receptacle. Keep your favorite calming oil in the car such as lavender or rose. When you put the drops in the diffuser, you'll be bathed in the natural aroma and immediately feel calmer.

EFT is a highly powerful technique for repatterning your brain. It's based on the ancient art of meridian systems in the body. EFT helps by taking the charge out of emotions that are held in the body. You can change your belief system about yourself through EFT! Check out www. eftuniverse.com and look for the PDF of core concepts under "How do I learn EFT?". I highly recommend starting small by using the karate chop point on the side of the hand, combined with the nine-point tapping system. Sheri Cooke of Totally Thriving offers a six-minute video on YouTube (www.youtube.com) to explain how to tap effectively. She's my favorite EFT tapper!

To get started with EFT, think of your issue and create a Set Up Phrase that you'll repeat. The structure is:

"Even though (issue), I deeply and completely accept myself."

For example, "Even though I get angry at my ex, I deeply and completely accept myself."

Or, "Even though I'm scared to divorce, I deeply and completely accept myself."

This becomes your Set Up Phrase that you'll repeat while tapping on the points as illustrated in The Basic Recipe. I've given you some charts to get started. Set aside 10 minutes twice a day and unhinge your old, unwanted patterns!

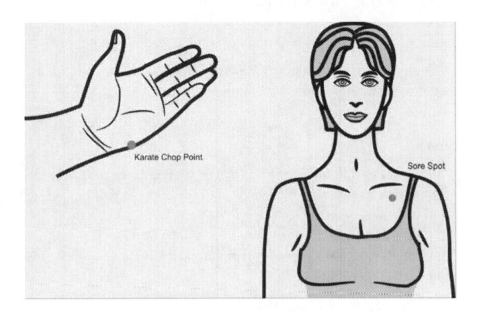

The Sequence. Now tap 7-8 times or so on the following points while repeating the Reminder Phrase. You may tap on either side of the body. "This *(problem)*"

...on the top of the head

...on the beginning of the eyebrow

...on the bone at the side of the eye

...on the bone just under the eye

...between the nose and top lip

...between the bottom lip and the chin

...just under the collarbone (in the angle created between the breastbone, collar bone and first rib)

...about 4 inches under the armpit (in line with a woman's bra strap, or a man's nipple)

Courtesy of www.eftuniverse.com

Keeping the Hope Alive

Bronze

Journal about what new activities you've created for yourself. Plan a special coffee with a girlfriend to celebrate all the new things you have in your life.

Silver

Journal about all the new things you've created. To keep clearing old habits, commit to learning EFT with a daily practice.

Gold

Complete the silver level activities, and plan a party to celebrate the woman you've become.

Affirmations

I enjoy the journey, stopping to smell the roses along the way.

I create change with ease and grace.

CHAPTER 10

Healing Medicine for the Heart
Three Forgiveness Rituals

*For some reason, we see divorce as a signal of failure, despite
the fact that each of us has a right, and an obligation,
to rectify any other mistake we make in life.*
~ Joyce Brothers, Author and Psychologist

The journey of forgiveness is like walking a labyrinth. You start along, forgiving a certain small thing, and before you know it, you're turning a corner and getting closer to a bigger issue. And it's too late to turn around, so you keep going, eventually turning another corner, looking away from the issue, yet closer, somehow, to the truth of it.

Forgiveness has gotten a bum rap. People often jump to the conclusion that they're going to have egg on their face as they apologize to someone. Forgiveness doesn't automatically mean you need to "literally apologize to someone". And it doesn't mean forgetting what happened either.

Wikipedia's definition of forgiveness is "the process of concluding resentment, indignation, or anger as a result of a perceived offense, difference, or mistake, and/or ceasing to demand punishment". It definitely takes a softening of the heart to be willing to forgive.

In the book *Oneness* by Rasha, the key to forgiveness is described as follows: "To release in total detachment, any care one may still be carrying, whatsoever, about the outcome of any drama revolving around that issue".

The gesture, then, becomes not one of forgiveness, which revolves around the issue of blame or non-blame for a perceived wrongdoing, but rather one of total transcendence of one's attachment to outcome.

The gold in forgiving is that we open our heart to receive more love. The benefit of forgiveness is that we receive healing for ourselves. We no longer carry the anger within our bones once it's released. There are different levels of forgiveness, sort of like peeling away the layers of an onion. Two of the layers are forgiveness of self and forgiveness of others. I find both are necessary to feel that the sorrow in the heart is lifted.

It's not uncommon to hear of women four years after a separation or divorce still grieving their loss. Now, four years may seem like a long time to many, yet when we're talking about a marriage of 10 years or more, well, that's a lot of history. When people have big transitions in their lives, healing takes time. Often the next piece of moving on is forgiveness of one's self.

Ready to Forgive

When Emily walked into my office after a vacation, I could see she'd made some strides. She was not as overcome with grief, and was actually smiling a bit now. She looked nicer than she did when I first saw her, and she had a new hairstyle. She was obviously taking greater care with her appearance. "I'm still not through," she said. After some exploration, she was able to see that what echoed for her was a sense that although she'd made it through the logistics of her divorce, she still needed to heal her heart with the balm of self-forgiveness.

She became aware that she was still holding on to grudges that were long since past. While in the grocery store, she would have flashbacks to the days of fighting with her ex over the groceries she brought home to her family. She and her husband had very different styles and thoughts about the best foods to eat. She realized she was still carrying anger towards him and blaming him for choices made years ago, even though they'd been living apart for three years! All of a sudden, she had a flash of insight that she didn't need to be carrying this angst. And it wasn't just about the way they shopped. This one small insight led Emily to other huge pieces of forgiving. She was able to clear the path for being in a new relationship by opening to forgiveness or her former relationship.

But Am I Ready to Forgive?

The timing of forgiveness is so different for each of us. While one woman may be ready to forgive small things one year after divorcing, another may not be ready for two to three years. Follow your own instincts and signs. Have you been hearing a lot about forgiveness lately? If the answer is yes, then it's probably time to do some of the work. Does the mere word forgiveness hit you over the head like a brick? If so, start forgiving slowly and allow yourself the freedom of time.

Interestingly, in 1988, the Gallup Organization found that 94% of those surveyed said it was important to forgive, but 85% said they needed some outside help to be able to forgive. If you're feeling unsure about where or how to begin forgiving, talk to friends or a coach and get support and ideas. It's likely others you know have been through a time in their life when they forgave others.

Some clients I see speak of needing to forgive themselves for the red flags they saw before they were married, yet decided to ignore. It's so easy to stay trapped in a place where you think someone *owes you* an apology. It's harder to admit that you need to forgive yourself for making a mistake at any point along the way.

Forgiveness is a muscle that when used, strengthens. And it can sound scary to even think of forgiving myself for certain actions or decisions made during my marriage. It's scarier still to think of forgiving my ex for his actions during our marriage—at least those I've been so darned mad about. So start practicing by forgiving small things that may have nothing to do with your marriage.

3 Rituals of Forgiveness

I've tried many forgiveness techniques and the three that follow are the complete trio that work for me. I start by Acknowledging the Gifts to pave the way. Then I move into Imagery for Releasing the Blame to take a closer look at what happened, accept responsibility, and lessen the emotional charge. Finally writing Letters of Grace allows me to send it up in smoke! Each exercise can be done for self-forgiveness as well as forgiving others.

1. Acknowledging the Gifts

This is the first place I typically start with clients who are looking to move on after their divorce, especially if they still talk a lot about their ex. It's so important to remind ourselves what the *gifts* of the past were. Often, as we move into divorce, there's a desire to only look at what went wrong. For deep healing to occur, however, we have to also look at what went well.

Make a list of the 100 gifts you received from your marriage (and I'm not talking about crock pots!). Start making a list of 20 gifts you received, then add to that as ideas come to you. And start with easy things, like we laughed together.

Here are some examples:

1. We enjoyed travelling together.
2. We have two great kids.
3. We bought our first house together.
4. We had nice vacations.
5. I had great sisters-in-law.

As you move forward in your list, it may get trickier. For example:

45. I learned to live with someone with a chronic illness.
46. I learned what it means to "dig deep" in myself.
47. I learned to trust.
48. I learned to stand up for myself.
49. I learned how to get through boredom.

Keep your list in a special, private place so you can add to it daily. Don't give up!!! Even if it takes you three months to get to 100, stay with the task. It'll be worth it.

2. Imagery for Releasing the Blame

Sometimes, forgiving might make you a bit nervous. In the next exercise, you'll start slowly and work from small pardons to larger, more emotionally charged pardons. You're going to reprogram your brain so you're okay with any past mistakes. Remember, when you made a mistake, it was in the past and you were in a different place than you are now. It was you in the past, not you as you are now.

Simply put, the exercise is to visualize an event three times while saying: **"I'm aware of, forgive, and learn from my mistakes."**

Here's how to practice the technique. Pretend you've spilled a glass of milk. It's pretty easy to forgive yourself *that*, isn't it? Everyone has spilled a glass of milk at one time or another.

Now visualize spilling the glass of milk and say to yourself: **"I'm aware of, forgive, and learn from my mistakes."**

Repeat this twice more. Visualize spilling the milk and saying at the same time to yourself: **"I'm aware of, forgive, and learn from my mistakes."** Again, visualize the event and say: **"I'm aware of, forgive, and learn from my mistakes."** Do this twice a day until there's no charge left when you bring up the memory of spilling the milk.

Then you'll move on to something bigger, with more heart attachment, like:

I'm sorry for the time I didn't call my mother back for two days.

I'm sorry for the time I wasn't available to my friend when she needed to talk

I'm sorry for the time I didn't stand up for myself when I didn't get the raise I deserved.

In each of these instances, as you're replaying them in your mind, notice how you felt at the time.

What did your body *feel* like?
- Was it tight?
- Hyper?
- Exhausted?

What were you feeling?
- Were you anxious?
- Fearful?
- Frazzled?

What other times have you felt that way?
- With my mother
- With my coworker
- With my son

Use the feelings as clues to remind you of other incidents to forgive. Each time say: "I'm aware of, forgive, and learn from my mistakes." Do this three times and feel it deeply within your body that you forgive yourself.

Once you've mastered a minimum of two scenarios of visualization that aren't directly related to your relationship with your ex, begin to forgive yourself for what happened with your ex-spouse. Remember to start with lesser charged events and work up to ones that had more emotional impact.

Setting aside a time period of 10 minutes in the morning and 10 minutes in the evening for one week can be a helpful practice in completing these exercises.

3. Letters of Grace

From time to time we recognize that we're angry with not only our ex, but our girlfriends, our family members, or our coworkers too. These grievances can add up, and I find that writing Letters of Grace helps me take the sting out of the relationship so I can be present for my family and friends.

To begin, find a time when you can unplug from the phone, computer, and children. Set aside a minimum of 30 minutes for yourself, with a pad of paper, your favorite pen, and a box of facial tissues by your side. Begin to write your letter, titling it Dear _____,. Then let the words pour forth. "I'm sorry for the part I played when . . . and I forgive you for . . ." Write down every little grievance you remember. Really give it all you've got. Feel the emotions of the entire experience and let them go. Release everything in this moment.

Then I suggest burning your letter rather than sending it to the other person. You'll be practicing self-forgiveness by not perpetuating the issue. Consider burning it in the fireplace or in a pot on your porch.

My client Emily had a deep experience of forgiveness while writing a Letter of Grace. "Imagine my surprise as I felt my heart opening and I realized I love him. I've spent the last two years hating every move he made through the divorce, and now I realize I love him. Not in the, 'Oh, let's get back together' way, but in the 'Wow, we're both parenting these kids so let's do our best together' way. It felt good to be through so much of that anger and hurt. I really just want to laugh about it. Of course, the divorce has been very disruptive and yet, I can see it's not the end of the world. I'm much happier overall and I'm so glad I forgave myself for all the petty things we sparred about over the years. I'm ready to date now."

I've heard from more than one client that they gained a newfound regard for their ex after completing this exercise. They talk about loving their ex for who he is now, seeing that he's grown and changed through the divorce too. It's a gift to be able to acknowledge that your ex is a great dad, or a great provider—a valuable person in his own right.

Even more powerful is gaining insight that I forgive myself for choices made during the marriage and during the divorce. Opening to and receiving self-forgiveness is the most powerful work we can do toward creating healthy relationships for ourselves now.

Whatever level of forgiveness you're working at, know you're not alone. Keep at it and the rewards will be priceless. You'll feel lighter and more loving. Imagine you're creating more space in your heart from which to love yourself and your family as you move through forgiveness.

Keeping the Hope Alive

Bronze

Begin a list of 100 gifts received from your marriage. Complete 30 items within the week.

Silver

Set aside 10 minutes in the morning and evening for your forgiveness exercises. Begin the list of 100 gifts received from your marriage. Complete 50 items within the week. Work up to an exercise of releasing the blame on an event with your ex. Complete that until the emotional charge is gone.

Gold

Complete the silver level as well and write three letters of grace.

Affirmations

I'm aware of, learn from, and forgive my mistakes.

I accept my new life in peace.

The End—or a New Beginning

Throughout all the ups and downs and the difficult moments of divorce, I hope you've been inspired—by reading this book and doing the exercises—to find the tenderness within to keep opening your heart. It takes great courage, determination, and patience to open to what's truly next in your life, from Source, God, or the Divine.

We surrender to the reality that we're in a divorce and do our best to make choices to walk through this period as a heroine rather than a victim. While dealing with intense grief, we endure separating and changing most of the relationships in our life. We get to redefine our priorities while finding clarity on what's next in our lives now. This is no easy task. We make it through the tough legal battles and find the time to do the work of forgiving ourselves and our partners.

I know at times your divorce may feel like it will never end. Or perhaps your divorce is running smoothly. Whichever is the case, know that you're not alone. Whether you still need to decide to divorce or do the work of staying together happily, there are resources available to keep you from feeling totally overwhelmed.

My wish for you is that you fully open to receive what's next in your life, whether that be a wonderful new relationship, a new calling in your career, or making lunches for your children and driving them around town.

About the Author

As a Relationship Coach, Lana Foladare, MA, guides people through the maze of their relationship changes, helping them stay consistent with their overall values, while making difficult choices that will affect the rest of their lives.

With a Master's in Psychology, Lana's goal is to help others come through their divorce as a whole person. She assists her clients in the areas of family changes, communication with the pending ex and lawyer, the legal process, creating social support, and positive emotional support. Clients particularly enjoy Lana's depth of skill in listening as well as her compassionate sense of joy and humor even during life's most difficult and critical moments.

Recommended Reading

Applewhite, Ashton. *Cutting Loose; Why Women Who End Their Marriages Do So Well*. New York: HarperCollins Publishers, 1998.

Berman, Clair. *What Am I Doing in a Stepfamily?* Secaucus, NJ.: Lyle Stuart, 1982. Ages 5 to 10.

Brown, Laurene Krasny, and Marc Brown. *Dinosaurs Divorce: A Guide for Changing Families*. Boston: Little, Brown, 1986. Ages 5 to 10.

Chodron, Pema. *When Things Fall Apart*. Boston: Shambhala Publications Inc., 1997.

McGuire, Paula. *Putting It Together: Teenagers Talk About Family Breakups*. New York: Delacorte, 1987.

Neuman, Gary. *Helping Your Kids Cope with Divorce: the Sandcastles Way*. New York: Random House, Inc. 1998.

Rosenberg, Maxine B. *Living with a Single Parent*. New York: Bradbury Press, 1992. Ages 8 to 13.

Schab, Lisa M. *The Divorce Workbook for Children*. California: New Harbinger Publications, Inc., 2008.

Venture, John, and Mary Reed. *Divorce for Dummies*. New Jersey: Wiley Publishing, Inc., 2009.

List of Values

1. Abundance
2. Acceptance
3. Accessibility
4. Accomplishment
5. Accuracy
6. Achievement
7. Acknowledgement
8. Adaptability
9. Adoration
10. Adventure
11. Affection
12. Aggressiveness
13. Agility
14. Appreciation
15. Assertiveness
16. Attractiveness
17. Audacity
18. Balance
19. Beauty
20. Being the best
21. Belonging
22. Boldness
23. Bravery
24. Calmness
25. Camaraderie
26. Candor

27. Capability
28. Certainty
29. Charity
30. Clarity
31. Cleverness
32. Comfort
33. Commitment
34. Compassion
35. Composure
36. Confidence
37. Connection
38. Consistency
39. Contentment
40. Contribution
41. Control
42. Courage
43. Creativity
44. Credibility
45. Curiosity
46. Daring
47. Decisiveness
48. Dependability
49. Depth
50. Desire
51. Determination
52. Devotion
53. Dignity
54. Diligence
55. Direction
56. Directness
57. Discipline
58. Discovery
59. Discretion
60. Diversity
61. Dominance

62. Education
63. Effectiveness
64. Efficiency
65. Empathy
66. Encouragement
67. Endurance
68. Excellence
69. Exploration
70. Fairness
71. Faith
72. Fame
73. Family
74. Fearlessness
75. Fidelity
76. Financial independence
77. Fitness
78. Flexibility
79. Focus
80. Freedom
81. Friendliness
82. Frugality
83. Fun
84. Generosity
85. Grace
86. Gratitude
87. Growth
88. Guidance
89. Happiness
90. Harmony
91. Health
92. Heart
93. Helpfulness
94. Honesty
95. Honor
96. Hopefulness

97. Hospitality
98. Humility
99. Humor
100. Independence
101. Insightfulness
102. Inspiration
103. Integrity
104. Intelligence
105. Intimacy
106. Intuition
107. Justice
108. Kindness
109. Knowledge
110. Leadership
111. Learning
112. Liveliness
113. Logic
114. Loyalty
115. Making a difference
116. Mastery
117. Maturity
118. Meekness
119. Mindfulness
120. Modesty
121. Motivation
122. Obedience
123. Openness
124. Optimism
125. Order
126. Organization
127. Originality
128. Passion
129. Peace
130. Perfection
131. Perkiness

132. Perseverance

133. Persistence

134. Persuasiveness

135. Power

136. Privacy

137. Reasonableness

138. Recognition

139. Reflection

140. Relaxation

141. Reliability

142. Resilience

143. Resourcefulness

144. Respect

145. Sacrifice

146. Security

147. Self-control

148. Sensitivity

149. Sensuality

150. Service

151. Sexuality

152. Simplicity

153. Skillfulness

154. Spirituality

155. Spontaneity

156. Success

157. Thoroughness

158. Trust

159. Truth

160. Understanding

161. Uniqueness

162. Unity

163. Usefulness

164. Variety

165. Victory

166. Vision

167. Vitality
168. Wealth
169. Willfulness
170. Willingness
171. Winning
172. Wisdom
173. Wonder
174. Youthfulness
175. Zeal